Getting the Most
FROM THE
BIBLE

G. STEVE KINNARD

Getting the Most
FROM THE
BIBLE

DPI

DISCIPLESHIP
PUBLICATIONS
INTERNATIONAL

Getting the Most from the Bible

ISBN: 1-57782-129-7

Cover Design: Chris Costello
Book Design: Chad Crossland

To Barry and Lin Beaty,
along with Brandon, Morgan and Jay Alexi

I have never met a couple who give more selflessly to the kingdom than the two of you.

Barry, your work ethic is beyond compare. You are a fighter. Your faithfulness and kingdom focus through four brain surgeries is inspiring. You are a hero to me.

Lin, thanks for being such a wonderful friend to Leigh. I remember a time when I had to take Leigh to the hospital for emergency surgery. You were the first person that I saw at the hospital. You have always been there for us.

The book of Proverbs says, "There is a friend who sticks closer than a brother [or a sister]" (Proverbs 18:24). You are those friends.

It is with deepest love that Leigh and I dedicate this book to you.

CONTENTS

Acknowledgments

Thanks to my family—Leigh, Chelsea and Daniel—for always loving me. You bring a smile to my face.

Thanks to the Aces and the New York ministry for allowing me to work on projects like this one.

Thanks to Steve and Lisa Johnson for all your encouragement through the years. You have blessed our lives. Thanks to Sam and Cynthia Powell and Sheridan and Debbie Wright for your inspiration. Thanks to Bob and Patricia Shaheen for your friendship. Thanks to John and Vivian Hanes for your constant support.

Thanks to Doug Jacoby, D.Min., Andrew Kitchen, Andrew Agerback, Win Linoto and Dr. John Oakes. Special thanks to Julie and Rex Geissler for your input and corrections on the manuscript and for your hard work and flexibility in getting it ready for DPI. Thanks to the DPI editorial staff for seeing the book on through to production. Special thanks to Tom Jones for his insightful suggestions. This is a better book because of Tom and the staff at DPI.

Finally, thanks be to God for his Bible and for the opportunities to be changed by it.

INTRODUCTION

Our Sacred Bible

"Take to heart all the words I have solemnly declared to you this day, so that you may command
your children to obey carefully all the words of this
law. They are not just idle words for you—they are
your life. By them you will live long in the land you
are crossing the Jordan to possess."

Moses, Deuteronomy 32:46-47

The Bible is like a telescope. If a man looks through his telescope, then he
sees worlds beyond, but if he looks "at" his telescope, then he does not see
anything but that. The Bible is a thing to be looked through, to see that
which is beyond, but most people only look at it, and so they see only the
dead letter.

Phillip Brooks, Bishop of Massachusetts

There is a living God. He has spoken in the Bible. He means what he says
and will do all he has promised.

James Hudson Taylor, British medical missionary

Whether you are a new Christian, a veteran Christian or a non-Christian who
wants to have a relationship with God, great Bible study is the key to getting
close and staying close to God. If you do not have a relationship with God and
are just beginning to learn more about him, then dig into the Bible and let it
teach you. If you are a part of the church and want to grow as a disciple, then
learning from the Scriptures is part of the process of spiritual maturity. If you
have been a disciple for years and years and desire to regain the edge you had
when you first became a disciple, then God's word can sharpen you. To say it
plainly: A steady diet of God's word is essential for spiritual growth. If we do not
have deep, meaningful Bible study, then we are destined to do poorly spiritually.

Appreciation Is Vital

The first key to having great, life-changing Bible study is to appreciate the amazing gift that God has given you by giving you his word. Be grateful that you have the living word of God at your fingertips. I went around my house and counted; we have sixty-three copies of the Bible. We have it in Hebrew, Greek, Russian, Hindi, Spanish, Latin and Samaritan.[1] We have children's Bibles, poet's Bibles, New Testaments, Old Testaments, small-print and large-print Bibles, computer versions, clothbound and leather bound versions, the Bible on video and on cassette—and everything in between. We have it in several translations: the Revised Standard Version, the New Revised Standard Version, the New International Version, the King James Version, the New King James Version, the Cotton Patch Version, the Jerusalem Edition, the American Standard Version, the New American Standard Version, the Singing Version, the Message, the TaNaK, the Living Oracles Edition, the Messianic Jewish Edition and many more. Personally, I could not possibly discard a Bible. The more used, marked and worn it becomes, the more valuable it is to me.

How much do you appreciate the Bible? If you are uncertain, then ask yourself a few simple questions: How much do I read the Bible? Do I know how to find my way around in the Bible? Is my personal study Bible underlined and marked up from use? Have I had studies in my Bible that have changed my life?

We need to appreciate the Bible. We do not hold many things sacred in the International Churches of Christ, which I think is good. Although many religious groups consider baptism a sacrament and have all types of traditions that surround it, we baptize people any place, any time. We baptize in baptisteries, water fountains, horse troughs, swimming pools, rivers, lakes, oceans, bathtubs or Jacuzzis. This is good. The place and time is not important. Each person simply must understand what is happening when they are baptized. We do not have any "Holy Grails" in the church. This is fine. If we were to adopt one holy, sacred item in our church, I suggest that it should be our Bibles. We need to treat the Bible with reverence, respect and awe.

Deep Convictions of Others

I will never forget a trip that my wife and I took to Bombay, India, in the late 1980s. We went there for an evangelistic campaign that the Bombay church hosted. We went across the enormous city of Bombay asking people to study the Bible. As I knocked doors, I met a young man from the Sikh religion, and we became good friends. We talked daily for the two weeks that I was there. When I was about to leave, he presented me with two gifts. One was a dagger from the Sikh holy temple in Amistar that was very special to him. Another was a copy of some of the sacred writings of the Sikh religion. His father was present when he gave me these gifts. His father seemed a little upset that his son gave me these gifts, which are considered sacred. His father asked me to do him one favor—since the writings were sacred to him, he requested that I not pack them in a suitcase containing shoes. To him, it was disrespectful to place the sacred writings next to items that are worn on the feet. This was his way of paying respect to the writings.

Jews also consider their Torah scrolls sacred. These scrolls are placed in special boxes in the front of their synagogues. They are not permitted to touch these scrolls with their hands. They have special poles that the scrolls are wrapped around so that they will not be handled. They read the scrolls by pointing at the words with special rods so that their fingers will not touch the parchments. When the scrolls become old and worn , they are buried in the ground as a sign of respect. Old scrolls of the Hebrew Scriptures were similarly treated. This is why, until the discovery of the Dead Sea Scrolls in 1947, the oldest copies of the Hebrew Scriptures were from the eleventh century AD.

I am not suggesting that we adopt this type of behavior with our Bibles. However, I was once offended by a person whom I saw using the Bible as a footstool. I asked him to not use his Bible to prop up his feet.

Appreciate the Sacrifices

We can take the Bible for granted. We should realize that it is a recent phenomenon for average people to have copies of the Scriptures. With Gutenberg's invention of the printing press in 1455, the Bible was mass-produced for the first time. Before then, most manuscripts were copied by hand. Gutenberg's Bible helped fuel the fire of the Protestant Reformation by putting the Bible into the hands of ordinary people. Although books were still expensive after Gutenberg's press was invented, more copies of books could be distributed than ever before in Europe.

For centuries the Catholic Church did not allow its members to read the Bible. They believed that priests alone should be permitted to read and interpret the Scriptures. John Wycliffe (1330-1384) was an English philosopher and theologian who pioneered the effort to get the Bible into the hands of ordinary people. His work helped prepare the way for the Protestant Reformation in England. In 1378 Wycliffe defied church tradition by translating the Vulgate, Jerome's Latin Bible, into English.

In 1380 Wycliffe began sending out his disciples, known as "Poor Preachers," to the countryside of England. Wycliffe believed in a direct relationship between God and humanity, without priestly mediation. He taught the primacy of grace in an individual's walk with God. He taught that people could follow the Scriptures and govern themselves without the need of popes or priests. Forty-four years after his death, still angry, churchmen had his body disinterred and burned at the stake.

Later, Martin Luther translated the Bible into German for a wide distribution, but the next major figure in the history of the English Bible was William Tyndale (c. 1492-1536). Tyndale studied theology at Oxford and Cambridge. He was determined to translate the Bible from the Hebrew and the Greek into English and wished to combat corruption in the English church by offering the Scriptures to the common people of England. The English church opposed this idea, so Tyndale traveled to the Continent and received the help of Martin Luther. Tyndale began printing his English translation in Cologne, Germany, beginning with the New Testament in 1526. Living in hiding for fear of the English churchmen, he eventually finished the English version of the Pentateuch in 1530.

Although the English religious authorities vigorously opposed Tyndale's translation, his version, along with Wycliffe's, did endure and became the foundation of the King James Version of 1611. Imperial authorities finally captured William Tyndale in 1534. He was imprisoned for sixteen months. He was tried and found guilty of heresy. On October 6, 1536, William Tyndale was strangled and burned at the stake.

Make Every Effort

May such stories inspire us to never take the Bible for granted. May we be forever grateful for those who have given even their lives so that we might have God's word so freely available to us. May their courage inspire us to go to the Bible, determined to get everything from it that God intends.

STEVE KINNARD, D.MIN.
New York City
May 2000

Note

1. I purchased the Samaritan Pentateuch on Mt. Gerezim in Nablus, Palestine, from a Samaritan grocer while I was living in Jerusalem in 1998. I am one of a handful of people with a personal copy of this book. I cannot read a word of it, but I love it just the same.

PART I

The Book of Books

1

Everything for Life and Godliness

I have found in the Bible words for my inmost thoughts, songs for my joy, utterance for my hidden griefs, and pleadings for my shame and feebleness.
Samuel Taylor Coleridge, English poet

The Bible is a wonderful, amazing book. It provides us with everything we need for life and godliness (2 Peter 1:3). If we need comfort, then we can go to the Psalms. When we need to see God in the flesh, we can go to the Gospels. If we do not understand God's grace, then we can study the book of Romans. If we want practical help on how to live godly lives, then we can turn to Proverbs or the book of James. If we want to be baffled and mystified, then parts of Daniel and Revelation can satisfy those desires. If we want to study Jewish history, then 1 and 2 Chronicles can inform us. Lessons in leadership can be gleaned from Nehemiah. Job teaches us about faith in the midst of suffering and pain. The Bible can be incredibly deep or plainly simple. It can inspire and it can terrify. There is something for everyone in the Bible. (See figure 1.)

Why Study God's Word?

Psalm 119 is an excellent psalm that extols the wonders of God's word. Take time to read this psalm and underline the phrases that laud the greatness of the Bible. Look at the different ways the psalmist mentions how beneficial the Scriptures are. Here are a few ways that are mentioned. Can you find more?

THE BIBLE IS ALWAYS THERE FOR US	
The Need	**A Good Scripture**
When in sorrow	*John 14*
When men fail you	*Psalm 27*
If you want to be fruitful	*John 15*
When you have sinned	*Psalm 51*
When you worry	*Matthew 6:19-34*
When you are in danger	*Psalm 91*
When God seems far away	*Psalm 139*
When your faith needs stirring	*Hebrews 11*
When you are lonely and fearful	*Psalm 23*
When you grow bitter and critical	*1 Corinthians 13*
For Paul's secret to happiness	*Colossians 3:12-17*
When you feel down and out	*Romans 8:31-39*
When you want peace and rest	*Matthew 11:25-30*
When the world seems bigger than God	*Psalm 90*
When you want Christian assurance	*Romans 8:1-30*
When you leave home for work or travel	*Psalm 121*
When your prayers grow narrow or selfish	*Psalm 67*
For a great invitation opportunity	*Isaiah 55*
When you want courage for a task	*Joshua 1*
For how to get along with fellow men	*Romans 12*
When you think of investments and returns	*Mark 10*
If you are depressed	*Psalm 27*
If your wallet is empty	*Psalm 37*
If you are losing confidence in people	*1 Corinthians 13*
If people seem unkind	*John 15*
If you are discouraged about your work	*Psalm 126*

Figure 1

Growth

To grow physically we need exercise, proper diet and rest. To grow spiritually we need prayer, fellowship and Bible study. Without Bible study, we will not mature spiritually.

> Your word is a lamp to my feet
>> and a light for my path....
>
> Uphold me, and I will be delivered;
>> I will always have regard for your decrees.
>
> You reject all who stray from your decrees,
>> for their deceitfulness is in vain.
>
> All the wicked of the earth you discard like dross;
>> therefore I love your statutes.
>
> My flesh trembles in fear of you;
>> I stand in awe of your laws.
>
> (Psalm 119:105, 117-120)

Obedience

Obedience does not come naturally. In Hebrews, the writer mentions that Jesus had to learn obedience (Hebrews 5:8). If Jesus had to learn obedience, think how difficult it is for us to learn it.

The Scriptures teach us the value of obedience. When we compare the path of the obedient heart to that of the disobedient heart, we should desire obedience.

> You have laid down precepts
>> that are to be fully obeyed.
>
> Oh, that my ways were steadfast
>> in obeying your decrees!...
>
> I have kept my feet from every evil path
>> so that I might obey your word....
>
> Your statutes are my heritage forever;
>> they are the joy of my heart.
>
> My heart is set on keeping your decrees
>> to the very end....
>
> Your statutes are wonderful;
>> therefore I obey them.
>
> (Psalm 119:4-5, 101, 111-112, 129)

Righteousness

By putting the Word into our hearts, we can keep sin out of our lives. The Bible is a powerful deterrent to sin. For this reason alone, Bible study should be a part of the everyday life of a disciple. This is also a great reason to memorize scriptures. If we hide the Word in our heart, then we will keep sin at a distance.

> How can a young man keep his way pure?
>> By living according to your word....
> I have hidden your word in my heart
>> that I might not sin against you....
> Turn my heart toward your statutes
>> and not toward selfish gain.
> Turn my eyes away from worthless things;
>> preserve my life according to your word....
> I gain understanding from your precepts;
>> therefore I hate every wrong path....
> Because I love your commands more than gold,
>> more than pure gold,
> and because I consider all your precepts right,
>> I hate every wrong path....
> Direct my footsteps according to your word;
>> let no sin rule over me.
> (Psalm 119:9, 11, 36-37, 104, 128, 133)

Knowledge and Wisdom

How can we learn more about God? How can we grow in our ability to make mature decisions as disciples? Knowledge and wisdom are gifts that God gives to those who diligently desire them, those who will spend time in God's word learning about God's heart.

> Your statutes are my delight;
>> they are my counselors....
> Teach me knowledge and good judgment,
>> for I believe in your commands....
> Your commands make me wiser than my enemies,
>> for they are ever with me.
> I have more insight than all my teachers,
>> for I meditate on your statutes.
> I have more understanding than the elders,
>> for I obey your precepts....

> The unfolding of your words gives light;
>> it gives understanding to the simple.
> (Psalm 119:24, 66, 98-100, 130)

Zeal

All of us have moments when we feel our zeal beginning to wane. We lose gratitude, stop sharing our faith and start complaining about all the sacrifices that we make as disciples. We take our eyes off the cross and start looking at the world. The Bible helps us refocus. It helps us pull things back into proper perspective. This increases our zeal for God.

> I am laid low in the dust;
>> preserve my life according to your word....
> My soul is weary with sorrow;
>> strengthen me according to your word....
> I will never forget your precepts,
>> for by them you have preserved my life.
> (Psalm 119:25, 28, 93)

Hope

Have you ever felt hopeless? Have you ever felt like you could not be fruitful, would never get married, could never be a loving parent? I am studying the Bible with someone who feels hopeless about becoming a disciple. He feels as if he just cannot change. This is a terrible place to be.

Satan wants us to feel hopeless. Fear and depression are his allies. When we feel hopeless, the Bible can inspire us to not lose hope. If Abraham and Sarah could have a child in their old age, then hope exists for us. If Jesus could come back from the dead, then anything is possible. If Saul of Tarsus could become the great apostle Paul, then any of us can change. The Bible gives us hope.

> May those who fear you rejoice when they see me,
>> for I have put my hope in your word....
> Great peace have they who love your law,
>> and nothing can make them stumble.
> (Psalm 119:74, 165)

A Disciple's Convictions

The primary responsibility and first priority of the disciple is to know and do the will of God. God has graciously given his will to us in the Bible. Some in this world look to church tradition for authority in religion. Others follow their own feelings. But the Bible gives us the exact will of God.

- Matthew 28:18-20
- 2 Timothy 3:16-17
- Jeremiah 10:23
- Psalm 119:105

For each disciple, the Bible is spiritual food that helps us grow to maturity, without which, we will die (Hosea 4:6-9).

- 1 Peter 2:1-2
- Hebrews 5:11-14
- John 4:31-34
- Matthew 5:6

The Bible is perfect and is the complete will of God revealed to humanity.

- Deuteronomy 18:15-18
- Jeremiah 31:31-34
- Hebrew 1:1-3
- John 16:12-13
- 1 Corinthians 3:18-20
- Galatians 1:8-9

Jesus Christ has been given all authority. We learn about Jesus through reading the Bible.

- Matthew 28:18
- 1 Corinthians 14:37

The Bible is God's powerful word.

- Isaiah 55:8-11
- Romans 1:16
- Hebrews 11:3
- Hebrews 4:12

The Bible can be understood. It is intelligible.

- Colossians 3:16
- 1 Thessalonians 5:27

It Matters Forever

We live in the Information Age. You can sit at your computer, surf the Web and instantly have information about an untold number of subjects. But listen to Peter's words as he quotes from Isaiah:

> "All men are like grass,
>> and all their glory is like the flowers of the field;
> the grass withers and the flowers fall,
>> but the word of the Lord stands forever."
> (1 Peter 1:24-25a)

The only information that will matter "forever" is what we find in the Bible. Learning to get the most from it is vital for us all. When William Tyndale was imprisoned because of his efforts to translate the Bible, he made a request for certain items. Part of this request reads,

> a warmer cap, a candle, a piece of cloth to patch my leggings....But above all, I beseech and entreat your clemency to be urgent with the Procureur that he may kindly permit me to have my Hebrew Bible, Hebrew Grammar, and Hebrew Dictionary, that I may spend time with that in study.

May we all have Tyndale's passion to spend time in the study of God's Word.

Part 2

The First Principles of Effective Study

2

Your Attitude Is the Key

When we study the Bible, attitude is crucial. What attitude do we need? George Mueller, a devotional writer, has written, "The vigor of our spiritual life will be in exact proportion to the place held by the Bible in our life and thought."

A Hungry Heart

> Therefore, rid yourselves of all malice and all deceit, hypocrisy, envy, and slander of every kind. Like newborn babies, crave pure spiritual milk, so that by it you may grow up in your salvation, now that you have tasted that the Lord is good. (1 Peter 2:1-3)

Those of us who have been parents understand how much babies love milk. When babies are hungry, they will let you know it. They will scream until they are satisfied. And when they are offered the bottle, they guzzle down the milk. It's as if they don't believe they will ever eat again.

How hungry are we for God's word? Those of us who live in the First World do not really know much about hunger. If you live in or have visited the Third World, then you have seen hunger. With hunger comes desperation.

I will never forget the sights and smells of Calcutta, India. Calcutta is a city of intense poverty. I remember driving up to a Hindu temple in Calcutta and watching as dozens of children surrounded our car with outstretched hands, begging for rupees. One girl especially caught my attention. She was eight to ten years old with long, straight, black hair that was dirty and matted together. She wore a threadbare dress that was probably once white, but seemed tan because it was unwashed. Protruding through her dress were the bones of her rib cage. In her eyes was a look of desperation. I could tell she didn't know where she would find her next meal. The hungry are desperate. Years later, I can still remember that look on her face.

Do you remember your hunger for the Bible when you first started studying the Scriptures? Do you remember how eager you were to learn? Remember the first time you saw the truth of what was being taught in Acts 2:38? Remember the first time you understood the importance of the Great Commission in Matthew 28:18-20? Remember the first time you saw the difference between worldly sorrow and godly sorrow in 2 Corinthians 7? How do you feel now when your evangelist asks you to open your Bible to Matthew 28? How do you feel when the Bible talk is on the Parable of the Sower? Do you think, "Oh, no, not again," or do you think, "Man, I love that story"? The Bible has the amazing, unique ability of always being fresh and new. If we keep an attitude of hunger, craving the Bible like a newborn baby, then the Bible will stay new and fresh for us. It's all a matter of attitude.

I heard the story once of a blind man who loved to hear God's word being read. Then he wanted to read the Bible on his own, so he learned how to read Braille for that sole purpose. One day, when he was walking out in his backyard, he tripped over something on the ground. Not knowing what it was, he felt around until he found what had tripped him. It was a blasting cap from a stick of dynamite. As he was fingering the object, trying to identify it, the blasting cap went off in his fingers. The explosion cost the man the use of his fingers. His greatest disappointment was the realization that he could no longer read the Bible on his own. So, do you know what he did? He learned to read Braille with his tongue. By reading Braille with his tongue, he could read the Bible for himself. That is hunger for God's word.

How hungry are you for the word of God? Are you desperate to learn God's word? Do you have a regular time each day when you sit down to study? Do you make sure that your study is uninterrupted? Do you study until you have been fed? Are you changing from your study? Are you just as excited to study the Bible today as when you first became a disciple?

An Obedient Heart

Oh, how I love your law!
I meditate on it all day long.

Your commands make me wiser than my enemies,
    for they are ever with me.
I have more insight than all my teachers,
    for I meditate on your statutes.
I have more understanding than the elders,
    for I obey your precepts.
I have kept my feet from every evil path
    so that I might obey your word.
I have not departed from your laws,
    for you yourself have taught me.
How sweet are your words to my taste,
    sweeter than honey to my mouth!
I gain understanding from your precepts;
    therefore I hate every wrong path.
(Psalm 119:97-104)

Once again, I would direct you to Psalm 119. It is an acrostic psalm: each verse begins with a letter of the Hebrew alphabet. The first eight verses begin with aleph, the next eight with the letter Bet'—until every letter of the Hebrew alphabet is used. This was a special literary device used to show how intensely the writer was concentrating on praising Scripture.

Psalm 119:97-104, quoted above, demonstrates that we are not just to read the word and analyze it, but we are to read it and obey it. The word of God demands a response of obedience. This is where most commentaries fail. Commentaries are great for analysis, but normally very weak at making the Bible practical and relevant.

Every single time we read the Bible, we should end our study by asking, "How do these scriptures apply to my life today?" "What am I going to change today from my study?" "How will I draw closer to God?" If we fail to take these steps, then we have failed to apply the Bible to our lives. The ultimate point of Bible study is to help us change our lives. We must read the Bible with obedient hearts.

A Disciplined Heart

"Ask and it will be given to you; seek and you will find; knock and the door will be opened to you. For everyone who asks receives; he who seeks finds; and to him who knocks, the door will be opened." (Matthew 7:7-8)

Sometimes great Biblical insight can leap right off the page. But more often than not, great insight comes from diligent, disciplined study of the Scriptures. We must approach the study of God's word in a disciplined manner. We should have both a place and a time that are conducive to study. We should let others know that our Bible study time is special and should be interrupted only in case of emergency.

If you have small children, then it can be difficult to find even five minutes that seem peaceful and quiet. Waking up early and staying up late seem impossible. Many people watch their time with God erode during the years of early child rearing. We must avoid this trap. When we raise our children, we must immerse ourselves in God's word. Find the time to study. As soon as your children are old enough to understand, let them know that your time with God is a priority, and teach them to respect your Bible study time. You will set a great example for your children to follow.

Imagine if you studied your Bible every day for five years. Imagine if you worked through the Bible each year of those five years. Imagine that you marked your Bible, underscoring phrases and verses that inspired you. Imagine if you memorized one verse a week for five years. Imagine that during those five years you read outside material that supplemented and explained what you were studying in the Scriptures. Imagine applying to your life every scripture that challenged you or called you higher. Where would you be at the end of five years if you were to approach the Bible with this attitude? Imagine where you would be at the end of ten years. This approach to the Bible will reap great rewards. Now stop dreaming about it and do it! Use this book as a guide to greater, more disciplined Bible study.

A Teachable Heart

> The Sovereign LORD has given me an instructed tongue,
>   to know the word that sustains the weary.
> He wakens me morning by morning,
>   wakens my ear to listen like one being taught.
> The Sovereign LORD has opened my ears,
>   and I have not been rebellious;
>   I have not drawn back. (Isaiah 50:4-5)

We need to have teachable hearts. A teachable heart is a heart that is open to the three Cs: challenge, criticism and change. The popular author M. Scott Peck defines it as a willingness to revise one's "map of reality." Our map of reality is the way we perceive the world around us. Our map is influenced by our parents, our educational background, our environment and worldly influences, like movies, music, magazines and television. If we are not open to revising our maps, then we cannot change our characters. Change is necessary to be a disciple.

The three Cs are especially needed when reading the Scriptures. Whenever we read a scripture, we must ask three questions: (1) How does this scripture challenge me?; (2) How can I critique my life from this scripture?; and (3) What will I change from my study of this scripture?

Here are a few practical guidelines about being teachable.

Be open to learning from every situation in life. See all of life as an education (Proverbs 6:6-11). The wise person will learn any time, anywhere, from anyone. For example, we can learn lessons from the ant about hard work. William Wordsworth said that nature was his greatest teacher. Henri Nouwen, a devotional writer, lists two categories for learning in *Making All Things New.*[1] The first category is solitude. Under solitude he lists prayer, study, meditation, contemplation and nature. The second category is community. Under community he lists relationships, group studies, work and family. Are you open to learning from every situation in life?

Be open to criticism from every person. Don't worry about whether or not the person has the right to criticize you. Listen to what is being said. Comment on the criticism and thank the person for it (Proverbs 12:1). Saying "Thank you" to constructive criticism makes you open to learning from others. If you don't take criticism well, don't expect many people to approach you with ideas that can help you change.

Listen attentively (Proverbs 18:13). Paul Tillich, a twentieth century theologian, wrote, "The first duty of love is to listen."[2] Alan Loy McGinnis, in *The Friendship Factor,* lists these characteristics of a good listener:

- Good listeners listen with their eyes.
- Good listeners dispense advice sparingly.
- Good listeners never break a confidence.
- Good listeners complete the loop by restating what was just said.
- Good listeners show gratitude when someone confides.[3]

Are you a good listener? The French philosopher Voltaire said, "The road to the heart is the ear." Being a good listener shows love.

Learn to control angry reactions. Often it is the people we love the most who are hardest to listen to. Why? Because we want to be accepted—warts and all. Becoming upset by criticism is a sure way to kill openness in the people who love us. We must learn to control our reactions when we receive criticism.

Be approachable. Approachability is a key to effective leadership. Tell people that you want to know what they are thinking. Let people know that you need their help. Value the opinions of others.

Break the pride barrier (Proverbs 16:18; 29:23). Pride and a teachable heart are the antithesis of each other. They are like matter and antimatter. To have one, you must get rid of the other. Let's rid ourselves of pride and keep the teachable heart.

Always be on your guard against hardheartedness. Continually check your attitude about change. Check how many times you must be told something before you initiate a change. Be on your guard against subtly adopting the characteristics of the world (Proverbs 4:23). Worldliness can sneak into our lives so easily that we must be on guard against it at all times. How do we define success: nice homes, new cars, fine clothes, traveling the world? If so, then Jesus was unsuccessful. We need to be careful that the world's way of looking at things does not pollute our perspective as disciples.

Seek advice from wise men. Seek out spiritual people and ask them to challenge you and to help you change (Proverbs 12:15, 15:22).

 Take periods of time for self-examination and introspection. Keep a journal of the ways that you are being challenged and the changes you have undergone. Continually set goals for yourself. These will help you initiate openness and change.

A Changed Heart

These ideas about being teachable need to be applied in many areas, but we can be sure that if we don't have an overall attitude of eagerness to learn, we will not bring that spirit to our study of the Bible.

Each time we approach the Bible, we will be well served to remember the message from Proverbs: "Above all else, guard your heart, for it is the wellspring of life" (Proverbs 4:23). When our hearts are hungry, obedient, disciplined and teachable, the word of God will be indeed living and active in our lives.

Notes

1. Henry Nouwen, *Making All Things New* (New York; Harper Collins, 1981), 36.
2. Alan Loy McGinnis, *The Friendship Factor* (Minneapolis: Ausburg, 1979), 109.
3. Ibid, 109-116.

3

Handling Correctly the Word of Truth

The Bible without the Holy Spirit is like a sundial by moonlight.
Dwight L. Moody, North American preacher

A thorough knowledge of the Bible is worth more than a college education.
President Theodore Roosevelt, USA

Parents of schoolchildren understand the difference between studying and studying effectively. Children can sit in a room and say that they are studying when their minds are outside playing on the swing set or shooting basketball. This is not effective or efficient study time. To study effectively, they must bring their minds back inside the room and concentrate on the work at hand.

I am sure that all of us have experienced reading a page of the Bible only to look back and wonder what we have just read. We read words but did not grasp the meaning of those words. This is not effective Bible study. To study the Bible effectively, we must gain insight into what the Scriptures are teaching us. Effective Bible study is life-changing Bible study.

The apostle Paul challenges his young disciple of Christ, Timothy, by writing,

> Do your best to present yourself to God as one approved, a workman who does not need to be ashamed and who correctly handles the word of truth. (2 Timothy 2:15)

Let's take a closer look at this challenge:

- "Do your best" *(spoudason)*—This word implies zeal and eagerness. It means to take great pains or to make every effort. We know what it is to do our best in an athletic event or on our jobs. If we are interested in pursuing someone in marriage, then we do our best to help that person fall in love with us. The aorist active imperative of the verb implies persistent zeal. Are we doing our best in our Bible study?
- "Approved" *(dokimos)*—This word means "to be approved after an examination or after testing." How would we fare if someone tested us on our Bible study? Do we study with the attitude that God is examining our hearts?
- "To be ashamed" *(anepaischuntos)*—This word has the connotation that we should have no occasion to be ashamed. It implies confidence. Have you ever been ashamed of your Bible study or your Bible knowledge? Are you confident that you are a good student of the Word?
- "Correctly handles" *(orthotomounta)*—This word means to cut along a straight line or to cut a straight road. Thus the KJV renders it "rightly divide." Fritz Rienecker, a New Testament Greek scholar, comments, "The metaphor could be that of plowing a straight furrow or a road maker driving his road straight or of a mason squaring and cutting a stone to fit in its proper place."[1] We can imagine the hard work that goes into plowing a straight line or laying down a straight road. It takes planning and proper execution to achieve these goals. For us to correctly handle the Word will take planning, execution and hard work as well.

How effective is your Bible study? Good Bible study takes planning. It will not happen by chance. You must sit down and answer certain questions—When? Where? What? Why? How long? When is the best time for me to study?

Generally, it is good to begin your day with Bible study. That way, you can think about the study during the day and apply it to your life. There are people who like to meditate on a scripture in the morning, but save their intense study time for when they settle down at night. After the children are asleep, they can spread out the Bible and a few books on the desk and attack the Scriptures. Do whichever works best for you. Choose a time when you will not be interrupted, and make sure that time is "sacred" and not to be skipped.

Sometimes we complain that we do not have enough time for great Bible study. When I feel this way, I remember a devotional piece by Michael Quoist, a French theologian, writing about the way to view time.

I went out, Lord.
Men were coming and going,
Walking and running.

Everything was rushing: cars, trucks, the street, and the whole town.
Men were rushing not to waste time.
They were rushing after time,
To catch up with time,
To gain time.

Good-bye, Sir, excuse me, I haven't time.
I'll come back. I can't wait, I haven't time.
I must end this letter—I haven't time.
I'd love to help you, but I haven't time.
I can't accept, having not time.
I can't think, I can't read, I'm swamped, I haven't time.
I'd like to pray, but I haven't time.

You understand, Lord, they simply haven't the time.
The child is playing, he hasn't time right now....Later on....
The schoolboy has his homework to do, he hasn't time....
     Later on....
The student has his course, and so much work....Later on....
The young man is at his sports, he hasn't time....Later on....
The young married man has his new house; he has to fix it up.
     He hasn't time....Later on....
The grandparents have their grandchildren. They haven't time....
     Later on....
They are ill, they have their treatments, they haven't time....
     Later on....
They are dying, they have no....
     Too late!.... They have no more time!...

In spite of all their efforts they're still short of time,
Of a great deal of time.

Lord, you must have made a mistake in your calculations.
There is a big mistake somewhere.
The hours are too short,
The days are too short,
Our lives are too short....

You who are beyond time, Lord, you smile to see us fighting it.
And you know what you are doing.
You make no mistakes in your distribution of time to men.
You give each one time to do what you want him to do.
But we must not lose time
    Waste time,
    Kill time,
For time is a gift you give us,
But a perishable gift,
A gift that does not keep....

I am not asking you tonight, Lord, for time to do this and then that,
But your grace to do conscientiously, in the time that you give me, what
you want me to do.[2]

We must find the time to study God's word. We make time for the things that we feel are important in life. Is it the same for spiritual matters? If we feel desperate to study the Bible, then we will find time to study it. The first principle for effective Bible study, then, is a sober attitude. We must realize how important this endeavor is. We must be committed to making the time to do it carefully, so that we will be approved by God as those who handle his Word with thoroughness and integrity.

Notes

1. Fritz Rienecker, *A Linguistic Key to the Greek New Testament,* translated by Cleon L. Rogers, Jr. (Grand Rapids, Mich.: Zondervan Publishing House, 1976), 642.

2. Michael Quoist, *Prayers,* translated by Agnes M. Forsyth and Anne Marie de Commaille (New York: Sheed and Ward, 1963), 96-99.

4

Preparation and Planning

In this chapter we want to look at some practical ideas to help you with good and consistent Bible study patterns.

The Importance of Place

First, find a place to study that will provide minimum interruptions. To have good Bible study takes concentrated effort. Interruptions are a plague to good Bible study. Do not study with the television on. Play only music that is conducive to study. If you study near a phone, do not plan on answering it.

Parents, teach your children that when Mom or Dad is studying the Bible, they should not be interrupted (except for emergencies, of course). We can teach our children to respect our study time. Indirectly, this will teach them that Bible study is valuable. Husbands and wives must fight for each to have great time in God's word. For example, take turns caring for the children to make sure that each of you has time to spend with God and the Bible.

Decide What to Study

It is important to find a topic that will inspire you in your Bible study. The topic should be something that will help you in your spiritual growth. People often come up to me and ask me what they should study. I usually reply by asking them if they have particular struggles going on in their spiritual lives at the time. Bible study that concentrates on something we are striving to change is the most effective type of study. Consider the following three types of Bible study.

Topical Studies

Many people love to study out topics in the Bible. If they are struggling with faith, then they will open the concordance and look up verses on faith. This can be a very beneficial way to study the Scriptures. A good friend of mine, Jim Brown, who is the minister of the church in the Westchester region in New York, likes to pick a particular topic and read through the entire Bible, paying close attention to that one topic. I have heard Jim develop some amazing sermons with this approach. I recently began a Bible study on perseverance and endurance this way.

Character Studies

I love how the Bible portrays the heroes of the faith as men and women who struggle with issues just like you and I. We see the great men and women of the Bible as they really were—good and bad, strengths and weaknesses, warts and all. We can learn great lessons from character studies in the Bible.

- Abraham   faith
- Timothy   the ministry
- Abraham   deceit
- Joshua   courage
- Joseph   righteousness
- Moses   leadership
- Esther   courage
- David   worship
- Ruth   loyalty
- Job   perseverance
- Paul   mission work

Study Whole Books

By far, my favorite way to study the Scriptures is to study book by book. By studying the individual books of the Bible, you learn how each book was constructed. You see how the author wrote to a particular group in a particular historical context. This allows you to learn how the Word meets our needs in every situation in life.

Studying the books of the Bible can be combined with a study of a particular need in life. (See figure 2.) Many of the Bible books contain a specific

YOU CAN FIND IT ALL IN THE BIBLE	
Topic	**Book**
Advice	*Proverbs*
Breaking the cycle of sin	*Judges*
Compassion	*Luke*
Courage	*Joshua*
Deceit of the world	*Ecclesiastes*
Discipleship	*Mark*
Divinity of Jesus	*John*
Evangelism	*Acts*
Faith	*James*
Faith through struggles	*Job*
Glory of the church	*Ephesians*
God is victorious	*Revelation*
God's everlasting love	*Hosea*
God's power	*Exodus*
God's providence	*Esther*
Grace	*Romans*
Gratitude	*Numbers*
Greatness of Jesus	*Hebrews*
Joy and gratitude	*Philippians*
Leadership	*1 and 2 Kings* *1 and 2 Timothy, Titus*
Lordship of Jesus	*Matthew*
Marriage	*Song of Songs*
Obedience	*Jonah*
Perseverance and endurance	*1 and 2 Peter*
Radical living	*Ezekiel*
Relationships	*Ruth, Philemon*
Righteousness	*Daniel*
Standing for the truth	*Jeremiah*
Worship	*Psalms*

Figure 2

theme or themes that run throughout the book. If this theme matches the need in your life, then you can study through that book, highlighting the material that meets your need.

For example, I see the books of the Bible listed in figure 2 as containing these themes. Perhaps a study of one of these books could help you with a particular need.

Pray About Your Study

> If any of you lacks wisdom, he should ask God, who gives generously to all without finding fault, and it will be given to him. (James 1:5)

If we are going to ask for wisdom, there is no better context in which to ask for it than in our study of God's word. Each time we open the Bible, we should begin with prayer—prayer for God to lead us to the scriptures that we need the most; prayer for wisdom to handle correctly the Word; and prayer to see the areas of our lives that need to change. We should pray to gain the conviction from our study needed to make lasting changes.

Prayer and Bible study go together like potatoes and gravy. In prayer, we talk to God. In Bible study, God talks to us. I have recently been contemplating why God tells us to pray for wisdom. In my twenty years of ministry, I have noticed that wisdom is not easily taught. It is more of an acquired attribute. I believe that God asks us to pray for wisdom because it is his gift to give. The more we concentrate and meditate on God in prayer, the more we are going to become like him—the more wisdom we will gain from him. Bible study also helps us to concentrate on God, thereby giving us wisdom. Together, Bible study and prayer are the perfect complement to each other. We gain wisdom from both. We should never begin studying our Bibles without praying to God for wisdom. Combine prayer with input from people who know you well and have suggestions about what you most need, and you will develop a plan that brings many benefits.

Read, Read, Read

It seems like a point too obvious to even mention, but it is important that we read the Bible over and over. The more we read it, the more we will gain from it. It is also important that we read the Bible in the right way.

The first time you approach a scripture, read through it once or twice without taking any notes. Then read it aloud. You may be surprised to learn that the Bible was written to be read aloud. The early disciples of Jesus did not have individual copies of the Scriptures; they read the Bible aloud in their gatherings. This is how they learned the Bible—from hearing it read. By speaking the Scriptures, we will remember more of what we read. Take time to read the Bible aloud so that you are reading it and hearing it read at the same time.

Next, read from several different translations. (We will look at the different English options in the next chapter.) Each translation will stress a different nuance of the passage. By reading through different translations, you will notice things that you would never notice by reading the same translation every time.

Observe and Take Notes

After you read through the passage several times and are familiar with its flow, read smaller sections slowly and carefully, taking notes and underlining key words and phrases as you go. People have different ways of doing this. Some use a notepad and record anything that seems important in this notepad. Some use colored highlighters to mark significant parts of the text. (I have seen Bibles that would make Joseph's coat of many colors jealous!) Other people mark in the margins of their Bibles. Find a method that works for you.

I have developed a favorite system over the years of marking and underlining in my Bible. I circle key words that I feel stand out in the text. I underline phrases or sentences that I feel deserve my attention. If it is a troublesome passage and deserves deeper study, then I put a question mark next to it in the margin as a note to come back and meditate on it. If it applies to Jesus and the cross, then I draw a small cross next to it in the margin. If I feel that I should memorize the scripture, then I put a star next to it in the margin. Later, I come back to those stars and memorize those scriptures. If it is a scripture that lends itself to being outlined, then I will start to outline it by writing one, two, three or four in the passage in appropriate places. If it is a passage that I believe can be worked into a sermon, then I will write the word "sermon" in the margin, and I will come back later and develop a sermon from it. The following is part of my system of underlining and taking notes. It helps me to approach the text in a logical, meaningful way.

As you read the passage, note these ideas.

The form of the passage. Is it a narrative passage, a psalm, a parable, an epistle or poetry? Each type of literature has certain characteristics. Try to determine what type of writing you are reading.

Key words and phrases. Note the words and phrases that seem important to you.

The setting of the passage. When was it written? To whom was it written? What prompted this text to be written? What is the historical context and geographical background of the passage? This information can often be gathered from looking closely at the text. At other times, Bible handbooks or commentaries might be needed to figure out these important questions. Often a good study Bible will provide this type of information.

Anything that seems unusual or out of the ordinary. If you do not understand what is being written, then note it. You might not be able to figure it out that day, but come back to it and meditate on it. The Bible was written to be understood. God is not a God of confusion, but of peace. He wants us to understand what was written. Spend time meditating on the passage to see if you can discern its meaning.

Two Missing Ms

Memorize

Why should we memorize scriptures? How important is it to memorize the Bible? The psalmist wrote, "I have hidden your word in my heart that I might not sin against you" (Psalm 119:11). Memorizing Scripture can keep us from sin. After Jesus fasted for forty days in the wilderness, Satan tempted him. Each of the three times he was tempted, Jesus returned Satan's tempting darts by quoting Scripture. If Jesus memorized scriptures and used them to fight temptation, then certainly we should do the same.

When you read the Bible, mark passages that you want to go back and memorize. Write these scriptures down on index cards and keep the cards with you. Look over the verses time and again to make sure that they are locked into your memory. By doing this, you will prepare your heart to withstand any temptation that Satan might send your way.

Meditate

Meditation is the duty of all.

Jeremy Taylor, Anglican minister

Hurry is not of the Devil; it is the Devil.

Carl Jung, psychologist

> I think of you [Yahweh] upon my bed,
>   and meditate on you in the watches of the night.
>   *Psalm 63:6, author's translation*

"Hurry up!"

"Let's get going."

"You're wasting my time."

"You don't have time to think."

"Why are you sitting around thinking when there is work to be done?"

These phrases are the mantras of our modern, active society. We want things done, and we want them done yesterday. The thought of meditating usually does not even enter our minds.

In the West, we do not value meditation in the same way that people do in the East. We are more action oriented. Meditation seems too passive for us. However, we must remember that the Bible is an Eastern book. The Bible talks often about meditation. It uses two different Hebrew words for meditation, and together they are used fifty-eight times. The psalmist wrote, "Oh how I love thy law! it is my meditation all the day" (Psalm 119:97 KJV).

What is meditation? Richard Foster, in his book, *Celebration of Discipline,* defines it as follows:

> Christian meditation, very simply, is the ability to hear God's voice and obey his word. It is that simple. I wish I could make it more complicated for those who like things difficult. It involves no hidden mysteries, no secret mantras, no mental gymnastics, and no esoteric flights into the cosmic consciousness. The truth of the matter is that the great God of the universe, the Creator of all things desires our fellowship.[1]

Meditation is the art of being still and thinking about God. It is an all–but-lost art in the Western world. Here are just some themes we can meditate upon:

- The love of God
- The death of Jesus (the cross)
- The value of a soul
- Walking in the steps of Jesus
- The trinity
- The peace of God
- God's patience
- Eternity

Do we take time to meditate upon God's word? Do we slow down enough to think about the great themes of the Bible? When was the last time you just thought and thought about one of the great themes of the Bible? Meditation takes time and stillness. Meditation means turning off the world and turning on your spirit and your mind. The goal of meditation is a changed mind and a changed heart. We take time out to energize our batteries by contemplating God. Then we go back to our activities with twice the energy and enthusiasm that we had before our time of contemplation.

Almost nothing brings a good result when it is done haphazardly. It is no different with Bible study: The more you pray and plan, the more effective your Bible study will be.

Notes

1. Richard Foster, *Celebration of Discipline* (San Francisco: Harper and Row, Publishers, 1978), 17.

5

Translation Appreciation 101

Although it would be ideal for every disciple of Christ to learn and use the original languages of the Bible (Hebrew for the Old Testament and Greek for the New Testament), this is not practical. Being able to read the Bible in the same language in which it was composed is a valuable asset. The fact of the matter is, however, that most people who have ever studied the Scriptures have done so by means of translations.

For example, the Septuagint was the study and preaching text used in the first century church. It is a Greek version of the Hebrew Old Testament. It was produced around 250 BC and is frequently inferior to the original text in Hebrew. But if the early church leaders could use a translation for their teaching and preaching, then so can we!

Translations are uninspired, and there is no English version of Scripture that is free of flaws. However, this does not mean that the person who studies from an English translation is endangered and liable to miss the saving truth of the gospel despite his best efforts to know the will of God. It is unlikely that the worst of translations could obscure the truth of salvation through Jesus Christ from the sincere student. But with the many translations available in English today, we have the advantage of being able to distinguish among them as to more and less reliable ones. We are also in a position to use more than one translation in our study so as to compare renderings.

As a basic study text, I recommend the use of these four major versions—the King James Version (KJV), the American Standard Version (ASV), the Revised Standard Version (RSV) and the New International Version (NIV).

King James Version

Many English translations were completed before the King James Version of 1611. As noted earlier, John Wycliffe published an English Bible based on the Latin text in 1382. William Tyndale, a graduate of Oxford, had a conviction that the Bible needed to be in the hands of the people. He published his translation of the Bible in 1525.

Building on the work of Wycliffe and Tyndale, the KJV, named after James I of England, was produced by a number of scholars from Oxford and Cambridge at the king's request. It is known as the "authorized" version, and even today you still find a few people who seem to think that God gave it to Moses on Mt. Sinai and that the use of any other version is heretical! The KJV is the most widely circulated piece of literature ever produced. It was translated in 1611 and reflects the literary excellence of its period in English history. However, the fact that it was produced more than 350 years ago also creates some obvious problems. Archaic words whose meanings are not known to the average reader in the twentieth century abound. A more serious criticism is that the KJV was produced from what we must now regard as an inferior textual base. The Greek text that the New Testament was translated from (Erasmus' third edition) was constructed from a limited number of late copies, which contained numerous copyists' errors and interpolations. (For example, Erasmus' text of Revelation lacked the last six verses. He supplied these by providing a Greek retranslation from the Latin.)

American Standard Version

In 1870 a committee of British and American scholars was organized by the Anglican church to revise the KJV. They published a literal translation in America in 1901 known as the American Standard Version. This version was produced in an effort to eliminate the archaisms of the KJV while taking advantage of the better textual base then available. The ASV attempted to render the text as literally as possible (word for word) while holding to the traditional tone of the English style represented by the KJV. Scholars acclaimed this version, but it never became popular with the Bible-reading public.

Revised Standard Version

An update of the ASV was done by scholars from forty denominations in the United States and Canada and became the Revised Standard Version of

1946 and 1952. This version represents an attempt to go from formal equivalence (word for word) to dynamic equivalence (thought for thought) as a translation principle. Formal equivalence seeks to replace each word or phrase in the donor text with a word or phrase in the receptor language. Dynamic equivalence strives for a thought-for-thought transfer from one language to another and pays particular attention to literary devices. The RSV was able to accomplish this better than any other translation to date. The New Revised Standard Version (NRSV), completed in 1989, is an updated version of the RSV.

New International Version

The New International Version, finished in 1978, follows the dynamic equivalence principle and is the most readable English version yet produced for modern readers. Its free style sometimes creates problems by rendering Greek words inconsistently and injecting interpretation into the text. If we are aware of these weaknesses and guard against them, then the NIV is a very useful Bible.

Many find it effective to combine the use of the NIV with the New American Standard Bible (NASB), a more recent revision of the ASV with far less archaic language. While not as readable as the NIV, it is useful when looking for the more literal translation of words or phrases.

Other modern English translations include:

- The New English Bible   1961
- Today's English Version/   1966, 1976
  Good News for Modern Man
- The New Living Translation   1998

To view these and a number of other translations and to compare passages from these versions, see the Bible Study Tools Web site found at http://bible.crosswalk.com/index.cgi.

My Personal Odyssey with Translations

I grew up reading the King James Version. At the time, I did not know that other translations existed. In fact, I did not know that the KJV was a translation. I just thought of it as "The Holy Bible." No one bothered to tell me that it was a translation from the Hebrew and Greek. I memorized Psalm 23, Psalm 100 and the Lord's Prayer in this translation. Even today, when these scriptures come to mind, I think of them in "King James" language. I love the language of the KJV. It is difficult to read, but it is flowery and poetic. There is a certain "other worldly" character to it. I drift back to this Bible of my childhood at times and enjoy it. For sheer poetic grandeur, the KJV stands alone.

When I went to college, the American Standard Version of 1901 was being used at my college, Freed-Hardeman in Henderson, Tennessee. They were devout believers in a literal word-for-word approach to Scripture, and the ASV was the most literal, word-for-word translation available at that time. While I was in college, I studied Greek and Hebrew. The ASV helped in my study of the Biblical languages. When I placed it next to the original languages, it was easy to follow the transition from the original into English. I do not particularly enjoy reading the ASV. It is too wooden and stiff (as is the more recent and more popular NASB). However, if I am working from the original languages, this translation is the closest to original text. Because of that, it has value for me in my study of the Scriptures.

The New International Version was published while I was in college. It first appeared only in the New Testament. Later, the book of Isaiah was released, and ultimately the entire Bible became available. I still have both a hardback and a leather bound single-column New Testament of the NIV from its first printing. When I initially read it, I was not impressed. To me, it was too modern and did not keep the dignity of the KJV or the accuracy of the ASV. I felt that it was too collegial—too familiar—and it used the modern vernacular in a way that put me off. So, I put it off! I packed it away and did not use it again until several years after I graduated from college.

When I was in graduate school at Southeastern Baptist Theological Seminary in Wake Forest, North Carolina, I used the Revised Standard Version. We were required to use the Oxford Annotated Study Edition of the RSV with the Apocrypha. This was the first time I ever read the Apocrypha. This gave me insight into the years between the close of the Old Testament and the opening of the New Testament. I loved the RSV.

Years before, I had used the RSV Harper Study Bible and found it to be one of the best study Bibles available. The notes in the Oxford Annotated were very liberal, but so was the school I was attending. I found that the RSV used a dynamic thought-for-thought approach to translation that was not as wooden as the ASV or as outdated as the KJV. But it also used beautiful, poetic, intelligent language—not the casual, common language of the NIV.

I continued my study of Hebrew and Greek in graduate school, completing my studies with a Master of Divinity with Languages degree. Then I could dig deeper into the original languages, relying less on the translations—this was a liberating feeling!

While in North Carolina, I became a part of a discipling ministry in the Raleigh area. This ministry used the NIV almost exclusively. Although I did not enjoy this translation, I began using it in my teaching and preaching because it was easier for people to follow along with me when I used it. I have continued to use this Bible through the years for this reason.

When I can, I read and study from the originals. I also read from various other translations including the Jerusalem Bible, *The Message,* the Poet's Bible, the New English Bible and several others. I have found that it is not important which translation we read; the important factor is that we read the Bible often.

Sure, some translations are better than others. However, I find that I can teach the message of Jesus and the way of salvation from any of the legitimate translations.

Although I enjoy a paraphrase like *The Message,* I have found another popular paraphrase, *The Living Bible,* to be full of misleading ideas.

I have found through the years that the more translations I use, the more I can gain from my Bible study. If you only read one translation, then you are only getting one approach to the original text. When you pick up another translation, new ideas will leap off the page at you. After you are familiar with one translation of the text, pick up another translation and compare the two to see what new ideas you can glean.

The bottom line for me is that I love to read God's word—in whatever version. This is why I studied Hebrew and Greek: this knowledge placed me one step closer to reading the text as it was originally written. Whether you read it in Hebrew, Greek, King James language, literal word-for-word equivalent, dynamic thought-for-thought equivalent, children's language, poetic language or ancient Sumerian, just make sure you read it! Remember the basic rule: *Read, read, read.*

PART 3

Digging Deeper

6

Principles of Bible Interpretation

The Word of God is in the Bible as the soul is in the body.
Peter Taylor Forsyth, Congregationalist theologian

When my family and I lived in Jerusalem for a year, I talked to many archaeologists who lived there. I talked to a geologist who was studying new material around Hezekiah's tunnel in Silwan. I spoke with the lead archaeologist of the land dig in Maritima Caesarea. I spoke with an archaeologist who oversaw the work at Bet' Shean during the summer months. Archaeologists often run into trouble when they dig. They discover material in particular layers of earth that contradicts a thesis that has already been proposed. When they hit this impasse, they have a proven method of finding a solution to the dilemma—they dig deeper. In archaeology, when you need an answer, you dig deeper.

The same adage can be used for Bible study. When you discover material in the text that you do not understand—dig deeper. But what tools should we use to dig deeper into the Bible? Below are four principles for Bible interpretation that will help you dig deeper into the text. Examples are included to clarify the principles. Have fun digging deeper!

Principle One
Interpret the Passage in Light of Its Context

A scripture should always be viewed in its context. An old country preacher once said to me, "A scripture taken out of context is a pretext." You can prove anything by taking scriptures out of context. You might have heard the story of the man who told God that he was going to open the Bible and point to three scriptures. Whatever those scriptures said, the man was going to prove his faith in God by immediately obeying those three randomly selected scriptures. On his first attempt, his finger fell on the scripture that says that Judas "went away and hanged himself." His second attempt fell open to "Go and do likewise." His third attempt fell to the fateful words, "What you are about to do, do quickly." The moral of this story: We "hang" ourselves when we take scriptures out of context.

Immediate Context

Upon reading a scripture, first consider the verses directly around the verse in question. This simple procedure will often help you make sense of the verse. Isaiah 58:11 could be used to say that when a person is a part of God's kingdom, their worries are all over. I have heard religious Israelis use verses like this to proclaim that the Israeli people are ordained by God to control the land of Palestine.

> "The LORD will guide you always;
>   he will satisfy your needs in a sun-scorched land
>   and will strengthen your frame.
> You will be like a well-watered garden,
>   like a spring whose waters never fail."

But when you consider the immediate context, you see that this promise is based upon the conditions stated in verses 9b-10. A careful reading of the immediate context can help clarify this verse:

> "If you do away with the yoke of oppression,
>   with the pointing finger and malicious talk,
> and if you spend yourselves in behalf of the hungry
>   and satisfy the needs of the oppressed,
> then your light will rise in the darkness,
>   and your night will become like the noonday."
> (Isaiah 58:9b-10)

Remote Context

The "remote context" is the context of the whole Bible. Consider how this passage or verse fits into the context of the rest of the Bible. Verses 16-17 of

1 Thessalonians 4 are often used as proof that there will be two resurrections: one for the righteous and a later one for the wicked. They are also used as proof that after the first resurrection of the righteous, a remnant will remain on the earth to face a time of tribulation. However, both the immediate and remote contexts of these verses must be considered.

In the immediate context, we see that Paul is addressing a question raised by the early church as to what would happen to their brothers and sisters who had already died. He states that the dead in Christ will rise first. Then all who are alive will be caught up with them in the clouds. In other words there will be one resurrection for the dead and the living. The dead will be raised first, then the living will be taken to meet God. As we read on in the next two verses (5:1-3), we see that on this same "day of the Lord," "destruction will come on them [the wicked] suddenly." In context, it is clear that the resurrection of the righteous and the judgment of the wicked occur on the same day, and that none are left on earth.

Now compare this passage with its remote context, the rest of the Bible. Jesus describes the resurrection in John 5:28-29 as being one resurrection of both the wicked and the righteous. Jesus says,

> "Do not be amazed at this, for a time is coming when all who are in their graves will hear his voice and come out—those who have done good will rise to live, and those who have done evil will rise to be condemned." (John 5:28-29)

The remote context of the passage supports a view that there will be one resurrection, not two. Therefore, 1 Thessalonians 4:16-17 must fit into the context of the rest of the Bible.

When we talk of looking at Scripture in light of the remote context, we are advocating letting Scripture be used to interpret Scripture. Here are a few guidelines:
- No passage of Scripture may be interpreted in such a way as to contradict another one.
- Always interpret the more obscure passage in light of the clearer one.
- Read the Bible extensively and study it regularly so that you will know its general ideas.

Perhaps the most important question to always ask when interpreting Scripture is the question of context: "What does this verse mean in its present context?" If you answer this question, most difficult verses will become clear.

Principle Two
Interpret According to the Correct Meaning of Words

Words can have several meanings. For example, the word "heaven" can mean the sky above us or it can mean the eternal home for the righteous. To interpret a scripture correctly, we must understand the correct definition of words in the passage.

Wrongful Redefining

Matthew 24:34 is a pivotal verse in understanding Jesus' teaching about the end of time. If you study Matthew 24 carefully, then you see that Jesus is answering two questions: (1) what will the signs be concerning the destruction of the temple in Jerusalem; and (2) what will the signs be for the end of time? Jesus answers the first question and then moves on to answer the second question. Verse 34 is the transition verse from question one to question two. Jesus says, "I tell you the truth, this generation will certainly not pass away until all these things have happened." A "generation" is a thirty- to forty-year time span. This is the way the word is consistently used throughout the Bible. All the signs that precede this verse—wars and rumors of wars, famines and earthquakes—apply to the destruction of the temple in Jerusalem that occurred in 70 AD.

Premillennialists want to apply the above signs to the second question concerning the end of time. They keep a constant eye on political developments around the world in an attempt to predict when Jesus will come and establish what they call his "millennial kingdom" on the earth. However, verse 34 gives them a problem. If the signs preceding verse 34 apply to the generation of the early disciples, then these signs cannot be applied to the end of time. Therefore, they redefine the word "generation." To them, "generation" becomes a dispensation of time. They reject the common, normal definition of the term (a definition that makes perfect sense in the context of the scripture) and redefine it to fit their doctrine. This is how word games can lead to false doctrine. But what are some guidelines for defining words?

Context, Context, Context

Often the context (words immediately preceding or following the word in question) will define the word. For example, 2 Timothy 3:16-17 in the KJV reads,

> All scripture is given by inspiration of God, and is profitable for doctrine, for reproof, for correction, for instruction in righteousness: That the man of God may be perfect, thoroughly furnished unto all good works.

What does the word "perfect" mean here? The common definition would be "faultless, without error." Does the Bible make us faultless? No—even with the Bible, we still sin and fall short of God's glory. The context defines the word. The verse reads, "perfect, thoroughly furnished unto all good works." In the context, the word "perfect" means that the Bible completely equips us to follow God. The NIV makes this clear by translating this phrase as "thoroughly equipped for every good work." As you can see, a look at the context helps define the word.

Parallelism

Hebrew poetry was built on parallel thought patterns more than on rhyme. The two most common types of parallelism in Scripture are synonymous parallelism and antithetical parallelism.

Synonymous parallelism is when two similar ideas are expressed together. One idea closely follows the other. The second idea clarifies and expands the first idea. For example, Psalm 7:13 states, "He has prepared his deadly weapons; he makes ready his flaming arrows." The first idea, "deadly weapons," is clarified and defined by the second parallel idea, "flaming arrows." Although this passage does not represent a deep doctrinal issue, it represents the mind of the Hebrew writers commonly expressing their ideas through parallelism.

Antithetical parallelism is when two opposite ideas are expressed in parallel thought. One idea helps define the other by stating the opposite of what has already been expressed. For example, Proverbs 15:1 reads, "A gentle answer turns away wrath, but a harsh word stirs up anger." The second idea expresses the converse of the first idea. In doing so, it helps clarify and define what is being stated in the first idea. The book of Proverbs contains many examples of this type of parallelism.

Important Terms

- "Hermeneutics" is the study of the principles that pertain to the proper interpretation of Scripture. In other words, hermeneutics is studying how to interpret.
- "Exegesis" is the practice of application of the principles of correct Biblical interpretation. This should be what we do whenever we study the Bible.
- "Exposition" is the communication of one's interpretation of Scripture to another. This occurs whenever we preach or teach the Scriptures.

Another example of antithetical parallelism is found in Genesis 29:17, where Leah and Rachel, the daughters of Laban, are contrasted. They are described in this way: "Leah had weak eyes, but Rachel was lovely in form, and beautiful." What does "weak eyes" mean? We do not generally use this term to describe people. If you look in the description of Rachel, you see the opposite of weak eyes, "lovely in form, and beautiful." "Weak eyes" was a euphemism for "not lovely." It was a delicate way to say that Leah was not the pretty sister; Rachel was.

Understanding Hebrew parallelism is very helpful in understanding Scripture. These are simple, easy examples that do not affect doctrine. But other examples can be used that show how an understanding of Hebrew parallelisms can help clarify important issues in Scripture. What is meant in the gospel of John by the word "belief"? In today's world, "belief" means to accept something as true. Does John have the same definition of "belief"? John uses Hebrew parallelism in John 3:36 to help clarify his meaning of "belief." The NIV renders the verse poorly in this way:

> Whoever believes in the Son has eternal life, but whoever rejects
> the Son will not see life, for God's wrath remains on him."

Notice the NASV rendering, which is much closer to the Greek meaning:

> "He who believes in the Son has eternal life; but he who does
> not obey the Son shall not see life, but the wrath of God abides
> on him."

John expresses his thought in antithetical parallelism—if you believe, you will have eternal life, but if you disobey, you will not see life. The antithetical parallel is between belief and disobedience.

Consistent throughout John's gospel is the idea that belief and obedience are one. To John, belief was more than just accepting something as true. Belief implied obedience. John 3:16 needs to be interpreted in connection with John 3:36.

> "For God so loved the world that he gave his one and only Son,
> that whoever believes in him shall not perish but have eternal
> life."

Understanding Hebrew parallelism helps us see how John used the word "belief" in his gospel.

Words in Remote Context

A concordance lists the use of words throughout the Bible. By using an unabridged concordance, you can define words by seeing how they are used in other parts of the Bible. (Just don't forget to pay attention to the immediate context each time.) Concordances are also great for doing word studies. A study on "grace" can be done by using a concordance to see how the word is used throughout the Bible. An exhaustive concordance will list every time the word is used. Zondervan publishes a good exhaustive concordance for the NIV. Computerized versions of concordances for the NIV and other versions are available from a number of sources. Such easy to use resources are great tools for helping us quickly locate useful information.

Hebrew and Greek Definitions

Since the Bible was originally written in Hebrew and Greek, with a touch of Aramaic here and there, an English dictionary is not very helpful in defining Biblical terms. It can help clarify the words in the translation of the text, but it will not demonstrate what was meant in the *original* language. Whenever I hear a preacher say, "I looked this word up in the dictionary and it means...," I cringe. The dictionary does not define Biblical terms. You must get behind the English to the original word in the Greek or Hebrew. How can a person without a working knowledge of Greek or Hebrew do that? It is not easy, but here are some helpful suggestions.

First, if you can learn the characters of the Greek and Hebrew alphabets, then you can use an interlinear translation that gives an English word for word translation underneath the original text. By reading through the English translation, you can find the original word used in a passage of Scripture. In John 3:16, "For God so loved the world," you can find that the word for "world" is *kosmon*. You can then look up *kosmon* in a Greek lexicon and find the different ways that word would have been used back then. Some of the more sophisticated electronic concordances give you the option of clicking on an interlinear translation after you have found the text in the your favorite English version.

Second, there are many Bible dictionaries that are keyed to English words. By using these, you can go behind the English to the original words in the Greek or Hebrew. One of the best is the four-volume set entitled *The New International Dictionary of New Testament Theology*. A good book to use for Hebrew words is the two-volume work entitled *Theological Wordbook of the Old Testament*. William Barclay's commentaries often provide good word studies based on the original languages. His volume of *New Testament Words* is also helpful in this area.

If you are going to do a word study, base it on the original word, not the English translation. A word should always be given its literal meaning unless other considerations forbid it. A good rule of thumb in Bible study is to always take the literal meaning of a verse first. If the verse makes sense with its literal meaning, then stand on the literal meaning of the verse. If the verse contradicts other verses or goes against a Biblical understanding of God and his nature, then find another meaning other than the literal one. Also, if the verse does not make sense when taken literally, then find another meaning. Consider this example from Luke 14:26. Jesus says,

> "If anyone comes to me and does not hate his father and mother, his wife and children, his brothers and sisters—yes, even his own life—he cannot be my disciple."

Almost every time that I have ever studied this verse with someone, they see the apparent contradiction here between Jesus' words and his character. Literally, Jesus is saying that his disciples must hate their families and themselves. But a literal interpretation of this scripture conflicts with everything we know about Jesus. So how do we explain the use of the word "hate" here? Jesus knew that the number-one pull against discipleship would be our closest relationships and our own selfish natures. If one does not get us, then the other will. Jesus is using a harsh, biting word to get us to wake up and pay attention to what he is saying. He uses a figure of speech called *hyperbole:* a dramatic exaggeration. He does not mean that we should literally hate (that is, be bitter, resentful or vengeful toward) our families or ourselves. Jesus everywhere teaches us to love—even our enemies. But he wants us to be aware of the strong pull of relationships and selfishness.[1]

Grammar

When you read the Bible, you read it in a particular language. Each language has rules of grammar. Knowing these rules can help you understand what has been written and can make interpretation easier. For example, the KJV translates 1 Corinthians 11:27 as,

> Wherefore whosoever shall eat this bread, and drink this cup of the Lord, unworthily, shall be guilty of the body and blood of the Lord.

In the context, Paul is writing concerning the practice of the Lord's Supper in the churches. Some have used this verse to prove that we should have a "closed" communion, namely, only disciples of Christ may take the communion. Can this verse be used to support this idea? Does the word "unworthily" describe the person taking communion? No, it does not. "Unworthily" is an adverb, not an adjective. It does not describe a person, place, thing or idea—an adjective does that. As an adverb, it modifies the verb. "Unworthily" describes *how* we take the communion. We must check our hearts and take the communion in the proper manner—focusing on the cross and the resurrection of Jesus. Other translations have proved helpful here by translating "unworthily" as "in an unworthy manner." This clarifies that the term is used as an adverb, not an adjective.

Principle Three
Interpret Scripture in Light of the Historical, Geographical and Cultural Context

Of all the principles, interpreting Scripture in light of the historical, geographical and cultural context of Biblical times is the most difficult to practice. It means going outside of the Bible itself and digging into texts about the history, geography and culture of Biblical times. This takes time and work, but of all the principles of Bible study, this can pay the biggest dividends. The Bible can come to life for us more than ever before. For example, when we understand how Abraham lived or the political climate of first century Palestine or the way a first century crucifixion was performed— this greatly adds to our understanding of the Scriptures.

Wrongly Colored Glasses

For the average Bible student today, probably the greatest failure is that we read the Bible with twenty-first century, Western glasses. The Bible is an Eastern book written between 1500 BC and 100 AD. To properly understand the Bible, we must turn off our twenty-first century, critical, historical, Western mind-set and enter the world of the ancient Middle East. John R. W. Stott, an evangelical writer, maintains that we need to transport ourselves back in time to understand the Bible. Life was very different in the first century AD. Their view of the world, of science, of history and of society was different. Certainly, their culture and everyday life was dramatically different from what most of us experience. If we understand these differences, then we can get closer to understanding what the Bible is saying in context.

A good illustration of how we tend to interpret the Bible by viewing it in our own context is the wonderful painting by Leonardo da Vinci of *The Last Supper.* Da Vinci portrayed the apostles as sitting around Jesus at a table in upright chairs enjoying a meal together. In the first century, people reclined on pillows to eat. The table was no more than eighteen to twenty-four inches above the floor. Da Vinci took the Bible story and made it fit into his context. We must do the opposite. We must abandon our context and enter the context of Biblical history.

Rich with Details

When we enter the context of Biblical history, the Bible comes to life. Consider the story of the Rich Man and Lazarus (Luke 16:19-31) in light of some details of history. In the story a poor beggar named Lazarus is placed at the door of a rich man's house. He desires to eat the crumbs that fall from the rich man's table. Historically, we know that some of those crumbs were the pieces of day-old bread that people used as napkins: the men raked them across their thick beards to clean their faces. They would take these pieces of bread and toss them under the tables for the dogs to eat. These are what Lazarus wanted to eat. Additionally the tables were eighteen to twenty-four inches above the floor. Lazarus wanted to crawl under one of those low tables to eat the crumbs and discarded "napkins" of the rich man— food left for the dogs. The dogs however were not interested in this food. They were more interested in licking Lazarus' sores. To eat the food, Lazarus would have to beat the dogs off him just to get at it. This is a pitiful picture of hopelessness. Yet the rich man showed no pity to Lazarus. He turned away from his need. The rest of the story shows, among other things, how judgment falls on such men.

Why do we need to spend time studying the sociohistorical settings of the Bible? The Bible was written in a cultural context. God chose to give universal truths by placing them in a particular cultural framework. We must be able to separate cultural phenomena from universal truth, but when we divorce the figures in the Bible from their cultural settings, it is like taking a play out of its proper historical context—the play can lose its meaning. John R. W. Stott notes,

> Although God's self-revelation is addressed to every man of every age and every country, each part of it was addressed in the first instance to a particular people of a particular age in a particular country. Therefore the permanent and universal message of Scripture can be understood only in the light of the circumstances in which it was originally given.[2]

History and Politics

What should we consider when we approach the Bible from a historical, sociopolitical point of view? We need to consider the history of the group to whom the passage was first addressed. We can better understand the ceremonies of the Israelites when we have a grasp of their historical background. The physical and material parts of the environment must be studied. Knowledge of the geography of the Holy Land is helpful and can add great insight to our study of the Scriptures. The language and the material culture (the homes, the objects in the homes, the tools for work and the implements for getting food, the clothing, the weapons, the means of transportation and other items which people used in their everyday existence) must be studied.

We should consider the political climate of the day. We should know whether Israel was free or in captivity in the books of the Minor Prophets. We should investigate economics—what was the economic situation of the Jerusalem church in the first century? We should look into the religious, moral and philosophical environment. All these aspects should be considered while exploring the historical settings for the stories of the Bible.

What principles should be followed when exploring the historical setting? Here are a few.

Cultural diversity within the Bible. When shifting from one book to another, we need to shift from one cultural setting to another. For example, we should be familiar with the change in Judaism during the Babylonian captivity. Judaism of the first century AD was vastly different from Judaism before 586 BC, when the temple was destroyed.

Biblical culture versus modern culture. We need to compare the culture of the text being studied to contemporary culture. By comparing these two distinct cultures, we will be ready to differentiate between cultural phenomena and universal truth. Sure, there will be some ambiguity and gray areas, but the serious student of the Bible must look for the universal truth amidst the cultural phenomena.

Unknown and confusing points. Look to external sources to clarify what an unknown term means. Look for direct, internal evidence in the writings to define specific cultural terms or to identify historical places and events.

Original, historical setting. Put yourself into the history of the text to determine what the passage must have meant to the people in its time. Only after doing this should you skip ahead to apply the scripture to your life today. This is a very important step. If we miss this step, then we will often misinterpret Scripture.

Seek to understand what meaning is relevant in today's culture, and make an appropriate application. If we are going to change our lives and influence our society with God's word, then we need to find the truth from the Bible and apply it.

Helpful hints. T. Norton Sterrett in his excellent book, *How to Understand Your Bible,* gives the following helpful ideas for identifying the cultural, historical setting of Biblical material:

- Learn the Bible. Read, read, read it. The more you are familiar with the whole Bible, the more you will have knowledge to help you in understanding it.

- Make notes as you read. Write down details about Bible characters, customs and features of the land.
- If you have a Bible with marginal references, use them.
- Use the map in your Bible to locate geographical points.
- If other books are available, use them. The first is a Bible dictionary. Many cultural items are explained in Bible dictionaries.[3]

Cultural Versus Universal Truth

One of the most important issues facing the Bible student is distinguishing between temporal, cultural phenomena and permanent, universal truth. God has chosen to give the revelation of his commands through men in a definite cultural setting. The student must separate a passage binding on cultural conditions from one that is universal. The student must separate cultural phenomena from universal truth, which means that he or she will have to investigate the cultural setting of scripture.

We must become aware of cultural phenomena in the Bible so that we do not make the cultural teachings of Israelite history binding on people today. How can the student distinguish cultural teaching from universal teaching? One resource the student must use in this process is common sense. Another good rule of thumb is to remember that when the justification of an injunction is related to cultural phenomena, then it is temporal in nature. When an injunction is given by transcultural language, it is permanent.

For example in 1 Corinthians 11, Paul uses cultural terms to relate a universal truth. He uses terms and phrases like "veil," "shaved head," "hair as glory"[4] and other cultural phenomena to show that there are distinctive roles that men and women must recognize in society. Men should be husbands and fathers, and women should be wives and mothers. When these roles become reversed, things fall apart.

The veil in first century Corinth was a long piece of cloth that sometimes dragged on the ground. It was similar to the veils that women in many Islamic societies wear today. It was used to show chastity and respect for authority. If we were to say that women must wear these today, then we must be consistent and wear the same type of veil that they were required to wear in the first century. Today's modern example of some denominational women wearing a napkin-size cloth square on the head is not closely similar to what they wore.

What about the length of our hair? The prostitutes of Corinth would not wear veils. They would often shave their heads or were forced to shave them. This became a sign of their profession. The women in the church should not have desired to look anything like those cultic prostitutes. Therefore, in first century Corinth, long hair was the glory of the woman. The same is true in some societies of the world today.

Paul is using cultural elements and customs (the veil and the length of hair) to teach a universal truth (women should be modest). Notice that he states that nature or custom teaches that hair is a glory and that society teaches that a veil is a glory. Both of these were binding only in first century Corinth. Today in most countries disciples live in, we do not have an equivalent custom for the veil or the length of hair, but the universal truth is certainly applicable to God's people. These types of cultural issues are important for us to understand as we read the Bible.

Principle Four
Look for a Practical Application of the Passage:
'What Does the Passage Say to Me Today?'

It is one thing to be told that the Bible has authority because it is divinely inspired, and another thing to feel one's heart leap out and grasp its truth.
Leslie Weatherhead, British minister and author

Imagine someone going to the doctor because of an ailment that causes tremendous pain. The doctor is unsuccessful in finding the cause of the pain and orders a series of tests on the patient in an attempt to find both the source of the pain and a remedy for it. After numerous tests, the doctor finally isolates the source of the pain and prescribes a pill that will attack the problem and relieve the patient. Now imagine if that patient, who endured the tests, the medical bills and the time spent with the doctor, neglected to take the pill and kept suffering. We would wonder if the patient was a masochist, a glutton for pain. It would seem strange for someone to undergo all the tests only to disregard the cure.

Similarly, it is ridiculous to spend time and effort in Bible study and then not apply the Bible to your life. I have sat through seminary- and doctoral-level Bible classes taught by professors who knew far more about the Bible than I will ever hope to know. They had knowledge of the Bible in Hebrew and

Greek. They had written books about the Bible. But for many of them, you would never have known that they had ever touched a Bible by looking at their lives. For them, Bible study was just an academic discipline. They failed to apply the Bible to their own lives.

Bible study must end with the application of the Scriptures. Ask yourself, "What am I going to change today from this study of the Bible?" During the day, take time to reflect on your Bible study and allow it to change your life. After all, the goal of Bible study should be a changed life.

Why Bother?

We live in a world torn apart by religious differences and schisms. Hundreds of denominational churches exist that teach different ideas about the Bible. Sometimes these are looked upon as trivial matters, but upon closer investigation, they are not so trivial. Churches are divided over teachings about salvation, baptism, the nature of God, the Godhead, the inspiration of the Bible, the work of the Holy Spirit and the importance of the church.

How do we find our way in such turbulent water? By being grounded in the Bible. If we know what the Bible says, then we can state with confidence what we believe in matters of doctrine. Paul told Timothy,

> Do your best to present yourself to God as one approved, a workman who does not need to be ashamed and who correctly handles the word of truth. (2 Timothy 2:15)

Jesus said, "You will know the truth, and the truth will set you free" (John 8:32). He also said,

> "There is a judge for the one who rejects me and does not accept my words; that very word which I spoke will condemn him at the last day." (John 12:48)

We can draw three conclusions from these verses. First, there is a correct and an incorrect way to handle the word of truth. We must be careful to handle it correctly. Second, we *can* know the truth. Third, the Scriptures are applicable to us because we will be judged by them (also, Acts 17:30-31). Since the word of Jesus will judge us on the last day, doesn't it make sense to live by his word every day?

Notes

1. A popular explanation of this passage by disciples is that the Greek word here for "hate" means "to love less." This is not true. The comparison of this text with Matthew 10:37 would lead to that conclusion, but in Luke 14 Jesus is using the normal word for "hate" but in a hyperbolic manner.

2. John R. W. Stott, *Understanding the Bible* (Minneapolis: World Wide Publication, 1972), 224.

3. T. Norton Sterrett, *How to Understand Your Bible* (Downers Grove, Illinois: Inter-Varsity Press, 1973), 81.

4. These particular terms are from my own translation.

7
Prophecy and Proverbs

As we examine the principles of interpretation, I want to use this chapter to look at two special types of literature that we find in the Bible and to consider the unique way in which we must deal with each. The first is prophecy; the second is proverbs.

Studying Prophecy

One area of Biblical study that seems extra difficult for people today is the study of prophecy. So much is being written about end-of-time prophecy that many people are confused. To correctly engage in the study of prophecy, there are several important issues to understand.

First Things First

Realize that the term "prophet" in the Bible means one who speaks the will or word of God (for example: Deuteronomy 18:17-18, Judges 6:8). He or she gives revelation from God to humanity. This revelation might be directed toward the past, present or future. The majority of prophecy found in the Bible was given to help people in their present condition. While prophecy is sometimes predictive in nature, a small minority of prophecy in the Bible concerns the end of time.

Types of Predictive Prophecy

Realize that there are different types of predictive prophecy. Here is a list of five types of predictive prophecy and an example for each.

Immediate predictions or prophecy with immediate fulfillment in the same context. For example, Exodus 14:4 concerns the hardening of Pharaoh's heart against the Hebrews.

OT predictions fulfilled in the latter part of the Old Testament. For example, Joshua 6:26 predicts the death of an older son and a younger son while building the walls of Jericho. This was fulfilled in 1 Kings 16:34.

OT prophecy fulfilled in the New Testament. For example, Micah 5:2 contains a Messianic prophecy concerning the place where the Messiah would be born (Bethlehem). The fulfillment of this is described in Matthew 2:1.

NT predictions fulfilled in NT times. For example, Jesus predicts his death in Mark 10:32-34. Jesus is specific in the manner in which the chief priest and scribes would treat him. He would be mocked, spit upon, flogged and then crucified. After three days he would come back from the dead. This was fulfilled in Mark 14-16.

NT predictions as yet unfulfilled. For example, in 1 Thessalonians 4:13-18, Paul writes about the second coming of Jesus. This prediction still needs to be fulfilled.

Characteristics of Predictive Prophecy

Present or past tense may be used in speaking of a future event. For example, Isaiah 53 speaks about Jesus, but it uses the past tense. This is known as the "prophetic past." Prophetic past demonstrates that God sees history simultaneously. God does not foretell an event because he is going to *cause* it to happen, but because it is going to happen.

Either a direct prediction or a typological prediction. For example, Zechariah 11:12-13 uses typological prediction. The scripture presents the type, and the antitype is of Judas and the betrayal of Jesus in Matthew 27:9.

Conditional and unconditional. For example, Jeremiah 18:7-8 is conditional. If a nation repents, then God will not destroy that nation. Daniel 2:44 is unconditional. God will establish a kingdom that will never be destroyed.

Near and far fulfillment. For example, Habakkuk 1:5-6 contains a near fulfillment in the captivity of Judah in 536 BC and a far fulfillment in the liberation from sin, through Jesus, that Paul spoke of in Acts 13:38-41.

Common Sense Principles

1. Make a careful grammatical and historical study of the prophetic passage.

2. Ask to whom the statement was addressed.

3. Look for internal keys that can be found in the scripture. For example in Daniel 2:36-38, Daniel established that Nebuchadnezzar is the "king of kings" in his dream. Therefore, everything should be interpreted following this key given by Daniel. Another example is Matthew 24:36—in speaking of the end of time, Jesus says that the Son does not know the day the world will end. Then why should we think that any mere human could predict that day?

4. Ask if the context suggests literal or figurative fulfillment. For example Isaiah 11:1-3, a messianic prophecy, points forward to a literal person who will bear these specific characteristics of messiahship: from the lineage of Jesse, possessing the Spirit of the Lord, possessing the Spirit of wisdom and understanding, possessing the Spirit of counsel and power and knowledge, and delighting in the fear of the Lord.

5. No prophecy can be given a meaning that contradicts a clear teaching of Scripture. For example, many premillennialists teach that the kingdom has not yet come. They teach that the kingdom is a millennial kingdom that will be established after the rapture of the church and the appearance of the antichrist, using passages like Daniel 9-11 and Revelation 14 and 16. The problem with this thinking is that an inspired apostle, Peter, clearly used "kingdom" prophecies in Acts 2 to say that the kingdom of God was being opened to all people on Pentecost. He refers back to Joel and Isaiah when he establishes the importance of what was occurring on that day. He refers to David, the great king of Israel, and mentions that Jesus is a greater king than David. If Jesus is king, then he has a kingdom, and his kingdom was established in Acts 2 on the day of Pentecost. Any use of prophecy that contradicts this clear understanding of Scripture is illegitimate.

6. The New Testament christological interpretation of Scripture is to be final. Often NT writers refer back to prophecy and give us the fulfillment of prophecy, saying that it directly refers to Jesus. When this is done, the interpretation of the inspired NT authors must be accepted. For example, in Isaiah 7:14 much has been made of the Hebrew word translated "virgin" in this passage. Should this be translated "virgin" or "young maiden"? Translations differ here. Is the verse predicting the

virgin birth of Jesus, or is it simply talking about the rise of a future king of Israel? Arguments can be made on both sides, but the key to understanding the Scriptures is to see how the NT writers viewed it. Matthew in no uncertain terms connects the verse to the birth of Jesus in Matthew 1:23. Since Matthew directly refers to what the verse means, we must take his view of the passage as inspired. No matter how the verse might have originally been used, Matthew gives us an inspired way to view it through his writings.

Studying the Proverbs

The book of Proverbs contains a special type of wisdom literature found throughout the Bible but collected in bulk in this one book. The proverbs are guidelines to righteous living. By following the proverbs, we can escape the destruction of wickedness and find the rewards of righteousness. These scriptures teach valuable lessons. Let's take a closer look at this special literary type—the proverb.

We hear many types of proverbs. The following serve as reminders to us of choices and consequences:

A penny saved is a penny earned.

Look both ways before crossing the street.

God have mercy on the man who doubts what he is sure of.[1]
Bruce Springsteen, rock singer

Mama always said, "Life is like a box of chocolates."[2]
Forrest Gump, fictional character

Proverbs were collected in Israel long before King Solomon became the voice of wisdom in the nation. But Solomon was the main advocate of this type of Biblical literature. They were collected under him and used in subsequent generations. All the nations around ancient Israel also collected and promoted such sayings.

A Sampling

R. B. Y. Scott, OT scholar, defines "proverb" as "a short, pregnant sentence whose meaning is applicable in many situations, with imagery or striking verbal form to assist the memory."[3] The proverbs stood as daily reminders of how to live a righteous life. In the book of Proverbs all wisdom stems from a relationship with God. The sayings serve as reminders of how to please God, how to be righteous. They offer practical advice or guidelines to be followed. Here are some examples.

Adultery

> "This is the way of an adulteress:
>   She eats and wipes her mouth
>   and says, 'I've done nothing wrong.'"
> (Proverbs 30:20)

Advice

> For lack of guidance a nation falls,
>   but many advisers make victory sure. (Proverbs 11:14)

> Plans fail for lack of counsel,
>   but with many advisers they succeed. (Proverbs 15:22)

Temper

> A hot-tempered man must pay the penalty;
>   if you rescue him, you will have to do it again.
> (Proverbs 19:19)

Laziness

> One who is slack in his work
>   is brother to one who destroys. (Proverbs 18:9)

Proverbs are especially helpful in counseling situations. Because they are so memorable, the proverbs offer just the right advice to people who need guidance. They are also helpful in the training of children. It is my personal conviction that part of the reason the proverbs were collected was so that they could be used in the Hebrew schools of the eighth and ninth century BC. Sam Laing, minister of the Triangle church, says that today Proverbs serves as a training manual for our children.[4] For example, here are some proverbs that can serve as a guide for our children.

He who sows wickedness reaps trouble,
    and the rod of his fury will be destroyed.
(Proverbs 22:8)

A perverse man stirs up dissension,
    and a gossip separates close friends. (Proverbs 16:28)

A generous man will himself be blessed,
    for he shares his food with the poor. (Proverbs 22:9)

An honest answer
    is like a kiss on the lips. (Proverbs 24:26)

Some of My Favorites

Perhaps by sharing with you some of my favorite proverbs and how I find them to apply today, you will be helped in your effort to make the proverbs useful in many other situations. There is no doubt that this is why they were written.

The wicked man flees though no one pursues,
    but the righteous are as bold as a lion. (Proverbs 28:1)

I'm sure we've all asked friends simple, innocent questions only to have them react in a harsh, surprising manner. Somehow, some way, we hit a nerve with them. Their guilty consciences cause them to react to a harmless question because this is how the guilty behave.

This proverb is an example of antithetical parallelism: the converse of the wicked is the righteous man, who is as bold as a lion. When we are righteous, we have power on our side. We are confident; we feel unbeatable. We walk with a bounce to our step. We hum songs like, "God is my father, Jesus is my brother, and the blessed Holy Spirit is my guide." We feel as if we could conquer the world. This is the feeling of righteousness.

Above all else, guard your heart,
    for it is the wellspring of life. (Proverbs 4:23)

Guard your heart (*Lav* in the Hebrew, and *kardia* in the Greek). The heart is the seat of the emotions. Nothing can get us off the right track quicker than our emotions. One great error of the Charismatic movement is that emotions are valued over intellect, experience over the written word of God.

How do you guard your heart? Know the Bible. Study the Scriptures. Ask advice from trusted people. Lean not on your own understanding (Proverbs 3:5). If we do not protect our hearts, then we are destined to bounce from one feeling to the next. We must rely on God's word, a constant in an unstable world, to guide us.

A tranquil mind gives life to the flesh, but passion makes the bones rot. (Proverbs 14:30, NRSV)

Serenity gives life to the flesh, but addiction and obsession make the bones rot—an addict's translation. I recently took a class in my doctoral program at Drew University entitled, "Addiction, Recovery and Spirituality." I came away from it with the realization that I have an addictive, obsessive-compulsive personality. Many of us do. We crave money, power, pleasure, leisure time and relationships. We cannot stop with just one thing—if there is a bowl of potato chips, we want the whole bowl. If there is a series of trading cards, we want the whole series.

The book of Ecclesiastes lists some items that can distract us: work, the newest model of anything, pleasure, laughter, wine, building projects, possessions, sex, inheritances, despair, power, oppression, youth, money and appetites. We can become slaves to the cravings of the flesh which makes the bones rot. It leads to useless pursuits—chasing after the wind (Ecclesiastes 4:6, 6:9). We must learn contentment. Only God can teach this as we surrender to him.

The man of integrity walks securely,
　　but he who takes crooked paths will be found out.
(Proverbs 10:9)

Integrity is an unknown commodity today. Robert Wuthnow, a Princeton professor, in his book, *Poor Richard's Principle,* gives results of a survey taken concerning ethics in business. His results are as follows:

- Eighty-seven percent of American business managers were willing to commit fraud in one or more of the cases presented to them. Most said that the fear of getting caught was the only deterrent to committing fraud.
- A majority of Americans rate the honesty and ethical standards of clergy, physicians and college professors as "very high" or "high."
- Only thirty percent give that rating to bankers.
- Only twenty-one percent to business executives.
- Only nineteen percent to members of congress.
- Only seventeen percent to real estate brokers.
- Only fourteen percent to stockbrokers.[5]

Disciples of Jesus must let their yes be yes. We must be people who can be counted on to keep their word and be responsible.

> Go to the ant, you sluggard;
>   consider its ways and be wise!
> It has no commander,
>   no overseer or ruler,
> yet it stores its provisions in summer
>   and gathers its food at harvest.
>
> How long will you lie there, you sluggard?
>   When will you get up from your sleep?
> A little sleep, a little slumber,
>   a little folding of the hands to rest—
> and poverty will come on you like a bandit
>   and scarcity like an armed man.
> (Proverbs 6:6-11)

Tony DiChiaro, a former New York City police officer and a friend of mine, offered me this wonderful proverb one day: "The more you do, the more you want to do. The less you do, the less you want to do." Laziness begets laziness. If you are lazy, then get up and do something. Turn off the television, leave the house and be productive. Simply make something happen. Start a job that must be finished, and finish it. Fight laziness at all costs.

He who mocks the poor shows contempt for their Maker;
whoever gloats over disaster will not go unpunished.
(Proverbs 17:5)

Many think the poor are poor because they are lazy. They mock them for this reason. I have heard people say things like, "If they would just get a job, then they wouldn't be poor"; "They are poor because they're lazy"; and "I've worked for what I've gotten. They should try a little hard work." In many parts of the world, poverty is a way of life. Some of the most industrious, hardworking people are poor. Many are poor because they were born in poverty and cannot find a way out. How arrogant of us, who have never been hungry a day in our lives, to mock the poor and sit in judgment of them.

Make plans by seeking advice;
if you wage war, obtain guidance. (Proverbs 20:18)

Victory comes from many advisors. When we fail to ask advice, we walk solo down trails that have already been traveled by many different people. Which is easier? Is it easier to learn by making mistakes or to learn from others' mistakes—thus avoiding the mistake? I will take the latter over the former.

How often do you hear, "If you would have just asked, then I would have told you that plan would not work"? If we have heard this, then we have failed to get advice. Advice can save us from many disasters. Let's become people who thrive from taking advice.

Like a city whose walls are broken down
is a man who lacks self-control. (Proverbs 25:28)

Leo Tolstoy, the Russian novelist, said, "There never has been, and cannot be, a good life without self-control." You can have a beautiful and expensive car that has been engineered by the finest car manufacturer on the planet, but if the gas pedal sticks when you floor it, it's just a wreck waiting to happen. In the same way, we can have great parents, a great education and wonderful travel experiences, but if we fail to learn self-control, then we are going to crash and burn.

Self-control starts in our brains. Francois Fenelon, a devotional writer, said, "If you are to be self-controlled in your speech, you must be self-controlled in your thinking."[6] To learn self-control, we must learn to control what we think. We cannot allow our minds to engage in thoughts of lust and greed. We must control the images that go into our minds so that we do not dwell on those images throughout the day. Self-control is an important part of discipleship.

> Gray hair is a crown of splendor;
>   it is attained by a righteous life. (Proverbs 16:31)

The older I become, the more I appreciate this verse. Aging is a part of life. You either grow old or you die—take your choice. We need to age with dignity. This verse helps us see that growing old can be a time of splendor. It's all in the attitude!

In my earlier book *The Call of the Wise,*[7] which is an introduction and topical index for Proverbs, I outlined some key principles to use when studying Proverbs. Here is a condensed version of those principles.

1. There is little to be learned by reading Proverbs all the way through without breaks. Each section, sometimes even each subsection, should be considered as an entity and studied as such.

2. A topical approach to Proverbs will greatly benefit the reader. Since many proverbs share the same theme, a topical study will provide a lesson of specific instruction on a specific issue. Poverty and wealth, the tongue, advice and correction, boldness, parents and children and discipline, for example, can all be studied topically through Proverbs.

3. Exercise your imagination and sense of humor while reading through Proverbs. The book stands as one of the most creative works in the

history of writing. A study of Proverbs should not be stale, but lively. These proverbs should entertain and delight us, but also move and motivate us. Most importantly, through the images conjured up by the proverbs, we should gain wisdom and learn to fear the Lord.

4. The great spiritual insights presented in Proverbs should never be neglected. Proverbs is packed with practical insight, but it is also full of spiritual wisdom. Proverbs can teach us some great lessons about the nature of God and his dealings with man. We learn what God likes and dislikes. The purpose is not to make you more clever but more spiritual.

Proverbs teaches one how to react and live in this material world, while reaching up to take hold of heaven. The modern believer will find ample direction in Proverbs about how to live life here and into eternity.

Notes

1. Bruce Springsteen, "Brilliant Disguise," *Tunnel of Love* (NYC: Columbia, 1987).

2. *Forrest Gump,* screenplay by Eric Roth (USA: Paramount Pictures, 1995). Based on the novel by Winston Groom.

3. R. B. Y. Scott, *The Way of Wisdom* (New York: Macmillan Publishing Co., Inc., 1971), 58.

4. From a personal conversation between Sam Laing and the author.

5. Robert Wunthrow, *Poor Richard's Principle* (Princeton, N.J.: Princeton University Press, 1996), 28.

6. Francois Fenelon, *Meditations of the Heart of God*, translated by Robert J. Edmonson (Brewster, Mass.: Paraclete Press, 1997), 33.

7. G. Steve Kinnard, *The Call of the Wise* (Woburn, Mass.: DPI, 1996).

PART 4

Scripture and History

One of the many divine qualities of the Bible is this, that it does not yield its secrets to the irreverent and the censorious.

James I. Packer, British theologian

Several years ago I read a delightful book by Robert Fulghum entitled, *All I Really Need to Know I Learned in Kindergarten*. The author talked, in a comedic but also serious way, about the foundation to life that he learned while a five-year-old in kindergarten. Personally, I never went to kindergarten. In the 1960s in Columbia, Tennessee, kindergarten was an option, not a requirement, and my parents opted out.

I did, however, go to Sunday school and to Wednesday-night Bible class. And every summer, Vacation Bible School was offered. There we sang songs like, "The B-I-B-L-E, that's the book for me" and "Booster, booster, be a booster, don't be grouchy like a rooster, and boost our Bible school." We learned the books of the Bible (in order, thirty-nine OT books and twenty-seven NT books) and the major and minor characters in the Bible stories. We had scripture memory and Bible quizzes. Looking back, I daresay that I knew more Bible when I was a ten-year-old than I did when I finished high school. The Bible was part of my everyday spiritual diet. I had no choice but to learn it. I'm not sure I would say "All I needed to know, I learned in Sunday School," but it was a good start.

Today, when I see adults struggle to find Nehemiah in the Bible, I am glad that I went to Sunday school. Because of Sunday school, I know that Jephthah was a judge of Israel and that Rehoboam was a king. I know that Aaron was the brother of Moses, and Miriam was his sister. I know that Paul went on three missionary journeys and that he was known as Saul of Tarsus before he became the apostle Paul. I am thankful for the Bible knowledge that I learned when I was a small child. (Parents today should be thankful for Kingdom Kids programs in our churches that are giving our children a great foundation.)

But many people have never had this opportunity. Many did not pick up a Bible until they were adults. They missed out on the stories of David and Goliath and of Moses and Pharaoh. They never read through a book of the Bible, much less through the entire Bible (something I did at an early age to win a prize in Sunday school). If you are one of the many who did not grow up reading the Bible, don't fret. It's never too late to learn. Start today. Decide that you are going to get your "GED" in Sunday school. Learn where the books of the Bible are located. Learn that Mark has sixteen chapters and that Matthew has twenty-eight. Learn the difference between a prophet and a priest. Start reading the Bible, paying attention to the major and minor characters. Read, read and read. You will be glad you did.

To understand the Bible, we must have a general understanding of the movement of God throughout the history of humanity. We must have a general sense of what the entire Bible says about God, humanity, sin, salvation and the kingdom. As we read particular sections of the Bible, we must be able to fit them into the whole of what the Bible says. Until we have this ability, we will feel a little lost in our Bible study.

This section will give a historical overview of the Bible. We will begin with Genesis and end with Revelation. We will give a sweeping review of God's dealings with humanity through the pages of the Bible. It is hoped that this will serve as a good outline of the Biblical text for those who are unfamiliar with it.

8

The Old Testament Period

I love the Old Testament, but not everyone feels this way. I remember a young disciple rebuking me after a Sunday sermon for preaching from the Old Testament too much. This person undervalued the Old Testament, which makes up seventy-five percent of our Bible. By answering a few simple questions, perhaps we can grasp the vital importance of the Old Testament.

What Is the Old Testament?

The Old Testament is a collection of books that were written and passed down through the nation of Israel. The earliest writings can be dated from 1,500 to 1,300 BC, and it is likely that many of the early OT stories were transmitted in oral form before they were written down. The Old Testament is written in Hebrew, the language of the nation of Israel, with small sections written in Aramaic. Incidentally, the number of books in the Hebrew Bible (twenty-four) differs from those in the current English one (thirty-nine) simply because the books are divided differently.

The word "testament" is really a misnomer. It comes from the term that Jerome (the fifth-century Bible translator) placed on the text. A better designation for the Old Testament would be the Old "Covenant," because it tells the story of God establishing a covenant first with Abraham and then with Israel. The Old Testament is the story of God acting in history to redeem humanity, and serves as a prelude to the new "covenant" (Jeremiah 31:31) that God would establish with all of humanity through Jesus.

Why Was the Old Testament Written?

The Old Testament tells the story of God's dealings with the Israelite people. The books of Moses (Genesis through Deuteronomy) recount the creation, the call of Abraham, the Egyptian bondage and the exodus from Egypt. The books of Joshua and Judges continue with the conquest of the promised land of Canaan. Joshua tells the story from the point of view of an immediate, total conquest of Canaan, and Judges gives the stories of the individual tribes who struggle to take and keep control of what God has promised them.

After the conquest, the story continues through the historical and the prophetic books. These books detail the rise of the united and divided monarchy in Israel. After the first three kings of Israel (Saul, David and Solomon), the kingdom is divided into two distinct governments: Israel in the north and Judah in the south. The northern kingdom of Israel is taken captive by the Assyrians in 722 BC, and the southern kingdom of Judah is later taken captive by the Babylonians in 586 BC. Prophets from both the north and south sound warnings of the impending doom to their countrymen. However, the warnings go unheeded, and the countries are doomed. But out of the wreck and rubble of captivity and destruction springs the hope that God will build a kingdom that will never be destroyed, that he will deliver his people once and for all. The expectation of deliverance is a theme used by the NT writers to speak about Jesus.

God is the major character who moves across the pages of the Old Testament. God creates the world and sets history in motion. God calls Abraham to become the father of the faithful. God delivers his people out of captivity by means of his servant Moses. God establishes his covenant with his people on Mount Sinai. God delivers the land of promise into the hands of his people. God allows his nation to chose a king and then establishes an eternal dynasty through David. God gives the prophets their message of doom and of hope for the people. The Old Testament is the story of God moving through human history to show humanity his love. In this way, the Old Testament is "theological history." It is history in the sense that God did move in particular times and places in history, but it is theological in that the historical events are used to present a portrait of God's love for his people.

The story of God's love is incomplete with the Old Testament alone. The ultimate portrayal of God's love for humanity comes in the person of Jesus. God plans throughout the Old Testament to demonstrate the ultimate gift of his love: the death of Jesus on the cross. In this way the Old Testament is a preview of the full, complete message of God as presented through Jesus.

Why Should We Study the Old Testament?

We need to study the Old Testament because it is difficult to understand the New Testament without it. How could we begin to comprehend the book

THE BOOKS OF THE OLD TESTAMENT			
Book	**Meaning**	**Date (century** BC**)**	**Theme of the Book**
Genesis	*origin*	15 or 13	Beginnings
Exodus	*a going out*	same	From bondage to covenant relationship
Leviticus	*things of the Levites*	same	Organization and instruction of priesthood
Numbers	*numbers*	same	The wilderness experience
Deuteronomy	*second law*	same	Restatement of the law
Joshua	*Yahweh saves*	13-12 (?)	Conquest of the land
Judges	*leader/deliverer*	11	God provides local leaders who fight for the land
Ruth	—	11	Friendship
Samuel	—	10	The beginning of the monarchy
Kings	*kings*	600-589	From Solomon to the exile
Chronicles	Hebrew: *events of the past* Greek: *things omitted*	400	Review of Israel's history
The Decline and Fall of Samaria at the Hands of the Assyrians			
Amos	*burden bearer*	786-742 Israel	Samaria must fall because of her sins
Jonah	*dove*	780-740 Ninevah	Universality of God's love
Hosea	*salvation*	745-715 Israel	Condemnation for idolatry and God's continuing love
Micah	*who is like Yahweh?*	740-710 Judah	Obey God from a true and trusting heart
Isaiah	*Yahweh is salvation*	742-698 Judah	Salvation is God's gift

Figure 3—*Continued on next page*

of Hebrews without some familiarity with the Old Testament? So much of the New Testament is built upon an understanding of what had already transpired between God and his people. When we read the catalogue of the

THE BOOKS OF THE OLD TESTAMENT—*CONTINUED*			
The Decline and Fall of Judah at the Hands of the Babylonians			
Zephaniah	*hidden by Yahweh*	621 Judah	The day of the Lord
Nahum	*consolation*	615-612 Judah	Destruction of Ninevah
Habakkuk	*embrace*	605 Judah	God will rule; the righteous shall live by faith
Jeremiah	*God establishes*	627-562 Judah	Judah will fall because of her sins
The Restoration Permitted by Persia			
Daniel	*God has judged*	605-530 The exiles	Prophecy of God's ultimate triumph
Ezekiel	*God strengthens*	592-570 The exiles	The sure destruction of Jerusalem and the reestablishment of Israel
Haggai	*the festive one*	536 Israel	Revive true worship; rebuild the temple
Zechariah	*he whom God remembers*	520-516 Israel	Rebuke for complacency and hypocrisy
Malachi	*my messenger*	445-432 Israel	Rebuke for complacency and hypocrisy
Prophets of Indefinite Date			
Joel	*Yahweh is God*	Judah	Repent—the day of the Lord is at hand
Obadiah	*the servant of Yahweh*	Judah	Destruction of Edom

Figure 3—*Continued*

faithful in Hebrews 11, it does not have the same edge, the same passionate call if we don't know the stories of the people who are listed there.

The New Testament constantly points back to the Old Testament, saying that it is a fulfillment of what occurred there. When Peter preaches the first recorded sermon after the resurrection in Acts 2, he quotes from Joel 2, essentially saying, "This is being fulfilled in your presence today." He also connects Jesus with the greatest king of Israel, King David. But he notes that David's grave was still there in Jerusalem for them to visit; whereas, the tomb of Jesus is empty because he rose from the dead. Someone unfamiliar with the Old Testament might ask why Peter was connecting Jesus with David at all. Without understanding the Messianic implications in such a connection, the correlation is lost.

There are many valuable lessons that can be learned from the Old Testament. As a child, I went to Sunday school every week. I loved hearing the miracle stories of Jesus and about the ministry of the great apostle Paul. But what I loved most were the blood-and-guts, dirt-and-muck stories of the Old Testament. I loved the image of the little shepherd boy David facing off against the big, ugly, Philistine giant Goliath. I could picture David swinging the sling around his head while Goliath looked on in disbelief. In fact, this is what so many of the OT stories are about: belief and disbelief. Is God big enough to deliver his people out of the hand of the mightiest power on earth, the Pharaoh of Egypt? Can God topple the walls of Jericho with the blast of a trumpet? Can God bless Abraham and Sarah with a child in their old age? Can God cause the earth to stand still so Israel can finish off her enemy? The OT stories aren't always "nice" or "politically correct." They often present humanity at its worst and can be difficult to understand; but we must not miss out on the great lessons of faith that they teach.

We cannot properly understand the prophetic material of the Bible without an understanding of the Old Testament. Recently, I was flipping through the television channels when I stopped on a religious program about end-of-time prophecy with none other than Hal Lindsey. I remembered reading his book *The Late Great Planet Earth* in high school and being totally confused by it. Lindsey and other premillennialists base much of their teaching on apocalyptic sections of Daniel and Ezekiel. The only way to understand what is being taught is to study these OT texts. By understanding them, we will have a greater appreciation for the kingdom of God and its place in history. Otherwise, we can devalue the kingdom and fall prey to prognosticators of the end time.

Understanding the Old Testament

My family and I had the great opportunity to live in Israel for the school year of 1997 and 1998. Living in the Holy Land afforded me the opportunity to travel around and see some of the great sites of OT history. I walked the streets of ancient Jerusalem, saw the walls of Jericho, visited the stables of Megiddo, hiked

PERIODS OF OT HISTORY	
Period	**Events**
Antediluvian	Creation to the Flood
Postdiluvian	Flood to the Call of Abraham
Patriarchal	Call of Abraham to the Descent into Egypt
Bondage	Descent into Egypt to the Crossing of the Red Sea
Wanderings	Crossing the Red Sea to Crossing the Jordan River
Conquest	Crossing the Jordan to the Death of Joshua
Judges	Death of Joshua to Saul's Anointing as King
United Kingdom	Saul's Anointing to Jeroboam as King
Divided Kingdom	Jeroboam's Kingship to the Fall of Samaria
Judah Alone	Fall of Samaria to the Fall of Jerusalem
Exile	Fall of Jerusalem to the Return of Zerubbabel
Postexilic	Return of Zerubbabel to the Close of the Old Testament

Figure 4

through the forests surrounding Dan, and suffered through the heat of Beersheba. Before I went, I did not have a clue how much seeing those sites would help my understanding of the Bible. (I'm not saying that every disciple must spend a year in Israel to really understand the Bible, although a week or ten days isn't a bad idea!) In order to gain a deeper understanding of the Old Testament, it helps to study the history, archaeology, geography and culture of the Middle East. A few properly chosen books can help us understand the social customs, religious rituals, historical background, living conditions and mindsets of the people of the Old Testament. This type of study pays great dividends.

But we should not try to understand the Old Testament without a proper understanding of the New Testament. I don't remember where I first heard the adage, "The Old Testament is the New Testament concealed; the New Testament is the Old Testament revealed." The NT writers always give the inspired interpretations of OT events. We should not attempt to interpret the Old Testament without consulting NT passages. Consider these three facts:

1. Jesus demonstrated to his disciples the interpretation of the Old Testament (Luke 2:15-46). When Jesus opened the Old Testament and said, "Today this scripture is fulfilled in your presence," he was the living breathing word of God giving the inspired fulfillment and interpretation to OT prophecy. The early disciples learned from the way Jesus handled the Scriptures. His approach to Scripture must have influenced the way they viewed the Old Testament.

2. The Holy Spirit led the disciples into all truth by means of miraculous spiritual gifts (John 14:3-21, 1 Corinthians 12-14). Not only were the early disciples influenced by the way Jesus used Scripture, but they also had the gift of miraculous spiritual gifts that helped them to approach the Scriptures in the proper way. These gifts were given to validate their interpretation of OT scripture.

3. We do not possess these same gifts today (1 Corinthians 13:8-10). Since we do not possess the same miraculous gifts as the early disciples, we must pay attention to how Jesus and his early disciples used Scripture and follow exactly their interpretation of OT scripture.

The NT writers use the OT material in various ways.[1] We can only determine their proper usage through study. Once we determine how the NT writers have used the Old Testament, then the NT usage must be seen as authoritative. This is especially crucial in our interpretation of OT prophecy.[2] We must also use the NT text as a gauge for interpreting the Old Testament. Both are vital for a full understanding of God's actions throughout history—neither can be fully understood without the other. The Old Testament is itself alive and vibrant; those viewing it as dull and meaningless are sadly mistaken.

Overview

The Hebrew Bible divides the OT material into three divisions: the Torah, the Prophets and the Writings. The first five books of the Old Testament are known as the Torah (Hebrew for "instruction") or the Pentateuch. The word "Pentateuch" is derived from the Greek words *pente* (five) and *teuchos* (scrolls). These are also called the Five Books of Moses or the Books of the Law. These books include Genesis, Exodus, Leviticus, Numbers and Deuteronomy. This section contains historical and legal material. The historical material relates to the story of humanity—Abraham's call and Moses leading

The Jewish Calendar

Sabbath: Every Saturday, the Sabbath was set aside as a day of rest. It began when the sun met the horizon on Friday evening. This was eventually standardized to 6:00 PM on Friday until 6:00 PM on Saturday.

Purim: February/March. Celebrated the deliverance of the Jews from the plot of Haman against the Jewish people as recorded in Esther. It was a celebration of joy.

Passover: March/April. The fourteenth day of Nisan. This was the oldest of the Jewish festivals. It celebrated the deliverance of the Hebrews from Egyptian captivity. The youngest member of the family asked, "What is so special about this night?" A narrative was then told about the Exodus of the Hebrews from Egyptian slavery.

Unleavened Bread: April. This feast was celebrated immediately after Passover, continuing for seven days. During this feast, the Jewish family was to remove all the yeast from the house. The Jews would remember the quick escape from Egypt during this feast.

Pentecost/Weeks: May/June. This was celebrated fifty days after Passover. It was a thanksgiving festival for the harvest of early grain. The feast was celebrated by the making of loaves of bread. The Jews also honored the law and Moses on this day.

Day of Atonement/*Yom Kippur*: September/October. This was a day of fasting and the most holy day of the Jewish calendar. It was an important day for the high priest. He would rise early and purify himself, pouring oil on his head. A bull was sacrificed on the great altar, and its blood was sprinkled on the ark of the covenant in the Holy of Holies. This was the one day of the year when the Holy of Holies could be entered, and then, only by the high priest.

Tabernacles/Feast of Booths: October. This feast was celebrated five days after Atonement/*Yom Kippur*. The Feast of Booths remembered the days when the Hebrews wandered in the wilderness for forty years after the escape from Egypt. It was a time of reflection and thanksgiving for the blessings of the year. The Jews celebrated the protection of God during this feast. They also thanked God for the autumn harvest. They built three-sided tents in their yards to remember how God led them through the wilderness. They hung the first fruits (grapes) on the tents as a sign of thanksgiving.

Dedication/Lights/*Hanukkah*: December. This feast originated during the intertestamental period (December 14, 164 BC). It celebrated the cleansing of the temple during the heroic activities of Judas Maccabeus. This festival is referred to in 1 Maccabees 4:56-59 and John 10:22-24.

Note: Two things can be learned from the Jewish festivals:

1. It was important for Israel to rehearse the mighty acts of God so that they would not be forgotten. They would reenact the Exodus or the wilderness wanderings.

2. Only one of the holy days was a day of fasting. The rest were days of celebration and festivities.

God's people out of Egypt. The legal material gives the essence of the constitution for Israel, including the Ten Commandments.

The Prophetic material is divided into the Former Prophets and the Later Prophets. The Former Prophets include Joshua, Judges, Samuel and Kings. The Later Prophets are the books of Isaiah, Jeremiah, Ezekiel and the twelve so-called Minor Prophets.

The Writings, or the *Hagiographa,* consists of eleven books, which cover a wide variety of styles. The book of Psalms is devotional and worship literature. Wisdom literature is found in Proverbs, Job and Ecclesiastes. The Song of Songs is a lyrical poem about romantic love. The book of Daniel tells the story of how God protected Daniel and his friends during the Babylonian captivity. Ezra and Nehemiah are memoirs giving important autobiographical and historical information of the postexilic period. The book of Chronicles gives a sweeping history of Israel from Adam to Nehemiah. Chronicles is the last book of the Hebrew Bible.

The Patriarchal Period—Creation to Sinai

The Patriarchal Period receives its name from the word "patriarch" or "father." During this period God spoke to humanity through the heads of the families, the patriarchs. Adam, Noah, Abraham, Isaac, Jacob and Joseph are major characters in this period. Beginning in Genesis 12, Abraham takes center stage in the patriarchal story. The material covering this period is primarily found in Genesis and Exodus. The book of Job is also placed in this context. Job is the story of one patriarch and his struggle to keep faith in the midst of terrible suffering. Job's faith is put to the test when he loses his possessions, his family and his health. His wife even tells him to curse God (Job 2:9). Job, however, struggles to find faith through the adversity. He ultimately clings to his faith, and God blesses him because of it.

Genesis means "beginnings." The story of Genesis begins with God. "In the beginning God created the heavens and the earth." We should not lose sight of the fact that of all the major characters of the Bible, God is the supreme character whom the Bible identifies. Soon after the Creation, sin enters the world. The story of the Bible is the story of God's attempt to win his creation back from sin. It is a long love story, a story of the love of the Creator for the creature. The Bible shows the extent to which God will go to win back his creation. Even as early as Genesis 3 there are hints as to the ultimate length to which God would go: the cross of Jesus.

Very quickly in Genesis, we see how deeply humanity sinks into sin: Cain murders his brother, Abel. Pride leads to the building of the Tower of Babel, where God confuses the languages of humanity. Wickedness increases until God decides to destroy the world with a flood. Noah stands out during this time as a beacon of righteousness. Through his righteousness, the world would be saved. After Noah, God initiates a special covenant with Abraham (Genesis 12). As God saved the world through Noah, he would now bless the world through Abraham.

Abraham was born approximately 2000 BC. God speaks to Abraham and instructs him to leave his home in Haran. Abraham obeys and journeys to Canaan (Palestine). God promises to make a great nation from the descendants of Abraham and to bless all the nations of the earth through him. The lineage of Abraham continues on through his descendants, Isaac and then Jacob. Jacob had twelve sons, one of whom was Joseph. The Biblical narrative concentrates on Joseph because he stands as a link with Egypt and explains how the Hebrews arrived in Egypt. Genesis ends and Exodus begins with the Hebrews in Egypt.

After Joseph dies, new Pharaohs rule Egypt without knowledge of who Joseph was or what he did for Egypt. These Pharaohs see the multitudes of Hebrews as a security risk. They enslave the Hebrews and use them for forced labor projects. In time, the Egyptians order the execution of Hebrew male babies. The Hebrews cry out to God for deliverance—and their cry is answered by the sending of Moses.

Though a Hebrew, Moses providentially grew up in Egypt as the son of Pharaoh's daughter. He fled to Egypt after killing an Egyptian who was mistreating one of the Hebrew workers. When Moses was eighty, God spoke to him from a burning bush, asking him to go into Egypt and deliver the Hebrews from oppression. Moses goes and squares off against Pharaoh by introducing ten plagues to convince the Egyptians to release the Hebrews. After the tenth plague, Pharaoh relents, and the Hebrews are allowed to leave.[3]

The Mosaic Age

What might be called the "Mosaic Age" begins when God establishes a covenant with the Hebrews at Sinai in Exodus 20. Through the Ten Commandments, God gives laws that set the covenant for Israel. Additional laws are given in the book of Leviticus. God establishes a priesthood, a sacrificial system and a calendar for festivals, and gives purity laws in this book. The laws were given so that the Hebrews would be a holy people—different from the nations around them. As they kept the law, God would bless them. This blessing would stand as a testimony that the God of the Hebrews was superior to the pagan gods of Egypt and Canaan. Because of the intense importance of these concerns in the religion of Israel, Leviticus came to be called by the Jewish people, *Sifra*, which means "the book."

The saga of the Hebrews' march to freedom continues in the book of Numbers. This book would be better identified by using its Hebrew title, *BeMidbar*, which means "in the wilderness." Because of their grumbling and complaining, the Hebrews are forced to wander in the wilderness south and east of Canaan for forty years. Of all the adults who left Egypt, only Joshua and Caleb are allowed to enter the Promised Land.

As the Hebrews stand to the east of Jericho and wait to enter the Promised Land, Moses prepares the people by giving them a "sermon on the law." This is found in the book of Deuteronomy, which means "second law." Moses summarizes his lifework as a leader in this book. He will not enter the Promised Land. Joshua has been chosen to take over the leadership of the Hebrews.

Joshua and the Promised Land

The record of the Hebrew people crossing the Jordan River to claim the Promised Land is recorded in the books of Joshua and Judges. Joshua gives the picture of a great army of God marching into the land, claiming victories in battle after battle. Judges pictures small tribal confederations attempting to oust local rulers from the lands they tenaciously hold. Both pictures are accurate. In fact, Moses said it would happen like this in Deuteronomy 7:22,

> The Lord your God will drive out those nations before you, little by little. You will not be allowed to eliminate them all at once, or the wild animals will multiply around you.

The Hebrews did march into Canaan and claim vast sections of the land. They also had to continue to fight smaller skirmishes to control the land.

Judges and Repeated Cycles

The book of Judges received its title because the contents of the book center on a group of leaders who serve as judges (leaders) of the people. (See figure 5.) The book records the history of the rather dark days between Joshua and the rise of the monarchy in Israel. Gleason Archer, an OT scholar, says, "The basic theme of the book is Israel's failure as a theocracy to keep true to the covenant even under the leadership of men chosen of God to deliver them from oppression."[4]

The story of the book of Judges follows an historical cycle. First, the people commit apostasy and leave the Lord, forgetting his laws. Then the people are oppressed by a foreign power. After a time of being oppressed, the people cry to God for deliverance. God hears their cry and sends a deliverer in the form of a judge of Israel. Then the cycle begins to repeat itself by the people leaving God and committing apostasy. The book is a micro-cosm of the hills and valleys of our own spiritual journey. How often do we forget the great things that God has done for us? We slip into times of apathy or even apostasy. The challenge is to break the Judges' cycle and stay on the mountaintop spiritually.

Ruth and Love Outside of Israel

The story of Ruth takes place within the time between Joshua and the rise of the monarchy. Seemingly written to explain how a Moabitess could be a part of David's ancestry, it stands as testimony of how God always planned for the nations around Israel to be influenced by God's demonstration of power within the borders of Israel. Even in the Old Testament, God grafted into the vine of Israel some Gentiles, showing his love for all nations. The story also presents a beautiful picture of loyalty and love among people, which

THE JUDGES			
Passage	**Name**	**Oppressor**	**Length**
Judges 3:7-11	Othniel	Mesopotamia under Cushan-rishathaim	40 years
Judges 3:12-30	Ehud	Moabites under Eglon	80 years
Judges 3:31	Shamgar	Philistines	—
Judges 4:1-5:31	Deborah (and Barak)	King Jabin of the Canaanites	40 years
Judges 6:1-8:32	Gideon	Midianites	40 years
Judges 8:33-9:57	Abimelech	Midianites	3 years
Judges 10:1-2	Tola	Midianites	23 years
Judges 10:3-5	Jair	Midianites	22 years
Judges 10:6-12:7	Jephthah	Philistines and Ammonites	6 years
Judges 12:8-10	Ibzan	Philistines and Ammonites	7 years
Judges 12:11-12	Elon	Philistines and Ammonites	10 years
Judges 12:13-15	Abdon	Philistines and Ammonites	8 years
Judges 13:1-16:31	Samson	Philistines	20 years

Figure 5

stands in stark contrast to the strife and lawlessness reflected in Judges. It also applies the law of Levirate marriage, that of the kinsman-redeemer.[5]

History Books—Kings to Exile

The books of 1 and 2 Samuel, 1 and 2 Kings, and 1 and 2 Chronicles all detail the history of Israel from the rise of the monarchy to the fall of the southern kingdom of Judah into the hands of the Babylonians.

Samuel stands as a transitional figure, leading Israel from the period of the Judges to the rise of the monarchy. He anoints Saul as the first king of Israel; Saul reigns for forty-two years. Although he began his reign with great promise, his arrogance and rebellion led to God's rejection of him as king. David is anointed by Samuel to replace Saul. David's descendents would continue to rule over Judah through the Old Testament, and the promised future Messiah would come from his lineage.

David began his rule of Israel from the southern city of Hebron, where Abraham was buried. After seven years in Hebron, David captures Jerusalem from the Jebusites and makes it the capital of Israel. From Jerusalem David begins to stretch the borders of Israel by waging war against her enemies. David is successful in building up a kingdom, establishing a dynasty and securing his house to provide the next king and the promised Messiah. Even with his faults, David would be looked upon as the king par excellence in the history of Israel. David was also known as a writer of psalms. The book of Psalms contains many of the psalms of David, which can be divided into several types.

- Hymns: 8, 19, 29, 33, 65, 68, 96, 98, 100, 103-105, 111, 113-115, 117, 135-136, 145-150
- Enthronement Hymns: 47, 93, 97, 99
- Songs of Zion: 46, 48, 66, 87, 122
- Laments of the Community: 44, 74, 79-80, 83
- Royal Psalms: 2, 18, 20-21, 45, 72, 101, 110, 132
- Laments of Individuals: 3, 5, 7, 13, 17, 22, 25-26, 28, 31, 35, 38-39, 42-43, 51, 54-57, 59, 61, 63-64, 69-71, 86, 88, 102, 109, 120, 130, 140-143
- Individual Psalms of Thanksgiving: 30, 32, 34, 41, 66, 92, 116, 118, 138
- Minor Groups:
  > Blessings and Curses
  > Pilgrim Psalms
  > Thanksgiving of the Community
  > Legends
  > Psalms Dealing with the Law
  > Prophetic Psalms
  > Wisdom Psalms

Solomon, David's son, succeeded David as king. God blessed Solomon with "wisdom and very great insight" (1 Kings 4:29) for which he was renowned the world over. Solomon consolidated the kingdom by making trade agreements with neighboring countries. His many marriages sealed treaties with countries that were once the enemies of Israel. Solomon had it all—wisdom, wealth, power, pleasure and fame. He reflects on all these in the books of Ecclesiastes, Song of Songs and Proverbs. Ecclesiastes speaks about

The Three Pillars of Judaism After the Exile

I. The Canon

The word "canon" means "a rod or measuring stick." Theologically speaking, it is the set of Scriptures which measure up to the standard of being God's word. The Jewish canon was made up of three divisions:

1. *Torah*—the five books of Moses, also known as the Pentateuch
2. *Neviim*—the collection of prophetic writings
3. *Kethubim*—the writings that included the historical and poetic books

Take the first letter from these three words to form *TaNaK*, or the Jewish Bible today.

The Septuagint was the translation of the Hebrew Old Testament into Greek. Legend states that seventy-two scribes worked seventy-two days to complete this translation. It was actually translated and collected between 250-150 BC. The Septuagint became the Bible of the early church.

II. The Synagogue

The synagogue has its roots in the Babylonian exile. It is never mentioned in the Old Testament. The word "synagogue" refers to a group of people who have been called to an assembly. With the destruction of the temple in 586 BC and the shutting down of the Jewish sacrificial system while in exile, the Jews formed smaller groups that met together to discuss the Torah.

Worship occurred at the synagogue on Saturday, Monday and Thursday. At least ten men had to be gathered for worship to start. The synagogue worship consisted of liturgy and instruction. The liturgy was (1) the *Shemah* (Deuteronomy 6:4-9), which served as a call to worship; (2) a prayer with uplifted hands; and (3) the chanting of the eighteen benedictions.

The instruction was comprised of (1) a reading of the Law and the Prophets; (2) a homily (sermon) on the passage read; and (3) a benediction.

The synagogue staff was made up of the president, who led the synagogue, and the Hazzan. The Hazzan carried out the orders of the president. He was the only person who was allowed to handle the scrolls. He also taught the children and administered flogging.

III. The Rabbi

In the Hebrew, *rabbi* means "my master." During the exile in Babylon the priest could not sacrifice, so scribes who accentuated the teaching of the law, rather than the practice of the law, replaced him. The scribes had to know many languages, and they were the most learned persons in the communities. They also became the best scholars of the law.

The role of rabbi grew out of the scribal sect. All the rabbis were scribes, but not all scribes were rabbis. The most learned scribes would gather a circle of students around them. Those like Hillel or Akiba became the rabbis. During the third and fourth century AD, the traditional interpretations of the rabbis were written down to form the Talmud.

the vanity of finding fulfillment in pursuing the pleasures of the world. After attempting to find peace through eating and drinking, building projects, sex and power, the writer concludes that true fulfillment can only come from following God and keeping his commandments (Ecclesiastes 12:13-14). Song of Songs is a love story extolling the pleasure and fulfillment of married love. Proverbs is a collection of wise sayings, many of these from Solomon himself.

After Solomon, the kingdom split into the northern kingdom of Israel, led by Jeroboam, and the southern kingdom of Judah, led by Rehoboam. The northern kingdom lasted for two hundred years. This kingdom never had a righteous king. It was more powerful than the southern kingdom, with three to four times more territory than the south. During the first sixty years there was war between the two kingdoms, followed by sixty years of alliance. The last seventy-five years were a mixture of alliance and war. Syria was the dominant force against Israel.

The Northern Kingdom

The dynasties of the northern kingdom can be divided into five periods.

1. *Heresy.* Jeroboam I to Omri, 931-874. Omri built Samaria, the capital of Israel.

2. *Apostasy.* Ahab to Jehoram, 874-841. Elijah and Elisha prophesy during this period.

3. *Dependence.* Jehu to Jehoahaz, 841-798. Israel was dependent on Syria.

4. *Material Prosperity.* Jehoash-Jeroboam II, 798-753. Jehoash has been looked upon as the greatest king of the northern kingdom. He ruled for forty-one years. Amos, Jonah and Hosea all prophesied during this time.

5. *Disintegration.* Zechariah-Hoshea, 753-732. Assyria conquers Israel and disperses the tribes into Assyria.

In 722 BC the northern kingdom of Israel fell to the mighty army of Assyria. The ten northern tribes of Israel were taken to Assyria and were assimilated into the Assyrian culture. The Assyrians were ruthless, harsh tyrants. After victorious battles, they deported their captives back to Assyria by using giant hooks, which they placed in the buttocks of their captives, chaining them together like fish on a string. This procedure assured two things—no one would escape and the captives would help each other along the march. Once in Assyria, the Assyrians forced their captives to forsake their religion and their culture. This was done so successfully that after the ten tribes of the Northern federation of Israel were taken into Assyria, they were never heard of again. They became the lost tribes of Israel.

The Southern Kingdom

The history of the southern kingdom of Judah can be divided into four periods.

1. A decline which was arrested by the first revival. Rehoboam to Jehoshaphat, 931-848.

2. A decline which was arrested by the second revival. Jehoram-Hezekiah, 848-698.

3. A decline arrested by the third revival. Manassah-Josiah, 698-608.

4. A decline without a revival. Jehoahaz-Zedekiah, 608-586. The Babylonians conquer Judah and destroy Jerusalem. Many Jews are taken to Babylon to live in exile there.

Exile to Postexile

The period of the exile in Babylon and the postexilic period is covered by the historical books of Ezra, Nehemiah and Esther. During this time the prophets Ezekiel and Daniel both prophesied. Ezra was a priest and scribe who was concerned with restoring proper worship to Jerusalem after the Babylonian captivity. His contemporary, Nehemiah, was concerned with the physical and political security of Judah. They worked together to rebuild the kingdom of Judah.

The Babylonian Exile

In 586 BC the southern kingdom of Judah fell to Nebuchadnezzar and the strong arm of the Babylonian Empire. Nebuchadnezzar marched into

The Temple Cultus

The temple was the central focal point of worship to the Jews. Their religious system was built around ritual. By the first century AD three temples had existed. Solomon's temple, built between 969-922 BC, was destroyed in 587 BC. Zerubbabel's temple was built in 515 BC, desecrated in 167 BC and rededicated in 163 BC. Herod's temple was begun in 20 BC and completed in AD 64. It was destroyed in AD 70.

The center of the temple cultus was the sacrificial system. Daily sacrifices were made between 9:00 AM and 3:00 PM. Lambs were sacrifices, and wine and bread were offered. The annual sacrifice was also offered at the temple in Jerusalem.

Jerusalem, destroyed the temple and took back to Babylon the temple treasury and the best of the Jewish people. He integrated these Jews into Babylonian life. Unlike the Assyrians, he did not ask the Jews to totally give up the religion of their fathers. He allowed them a sense of freedom and independence within the Babylonian framework. These became the Jews of the exile. They set up communities outside of the city of Babylon and kept their religion and culture alive. During this time the seeds of synagogue worship were planted. They did not have the temple or the altar in Jerusalem so they came together in small groups and read the Torah and discussed the law. Through these groups they kept Judaism alive. With the destruction of the temple in 587 BC, the Hebrew faith ended and the Jewish faith began.

Israel's Babylonian experience was that of an enforced exile, not a captivity in the sense of bondage (as in the Egyptian experience). Jeremiah notes that the exile would last seventy years (Jeremiah 25:11). This figure may be taken as a round number, or if one wishes to figure seventy years more exactly, this duration may be reckoned from Nebuchadnezzar's first incursion into Canaan to Israel's first return under Zerubbabel—or alternately, from Jerusalem's fall in 586 BC to the dedication of the rebuilt temple in 516 BC.

What lessons did Israel learn during the Babylonian captivity?

1. As a result of Israel's sin, the prophets of doom were proven right.

2. Israel learned the folly of idolatry, so that the restored people later were not threatened nearly so much by pagan religion.

3. Israel learned that she could serve the Lord anywhere.

4. Such distinguished later institutions as the synagogue may have had their origin in the exile.

Here are some facts about the exile.

- Prophetic warnings concerning the exile are found in Isaiah, Jeremiah and Ezekiel.
- Psalm 137—the people were disconsolate upon their first arrival in Babylon.
- Daniel was an inspired statesman at the Babylonian court; later, Esther delivered her people as a member of the Persian court.
- Jeremiah counseled the exiles to live peacefully in Babylon (Jeremiah 25 and 29).
- Ezekiel lived and worked among the exiled people.
- The exile furnishes the background for Ezra and Nehemiah (which describe the return from exile and the rebuilding of the temple and the walls of Jerusalem).

Palestine During Persian Rule

In 539 BC a Persian ruler named Cyrus marched into Babylon and claimed it for the Persian Empire. He thus became king over Mesopotamia, Syria and Palestine. Cyrus was even more lenient with his captives than the Babylonians. He allowed the Jews to return to their homeland in Judah. He issued an edict calling for the temple of Jerusalem to be rebuilt. He even provided funds for this venture. He called for the stolen temple treasures to be returned to the Jews and allowed them freedom to rebuild their city.

The prophet who served as a bridge between the Hebrew faith and the rise of Judaism during the Babylonian captivity was Jeremiah. At twenty, he saw a revival under Josiah in 621 BC. During this time he saw the nation of Judah recommit to God. In 604 BC, when he was forty, he saw his people taken into captivity. In 587 BC he witnessed the last deportation of the Jews into Babylon. The skilled workers and craftsmen were taken first, and the menial workers and slaves were taken last.

In 587 the temple was destroyed, causing a major crisis in the Jewish faith. Their faith became tainted with foreign influence. Jeremiah was fifty-five when he saw the temple destroyed. After the temple's destruction, the law was elevated. The study of the law replaced the practice of the law. The Jews in captivity did the best they could to hold onto the faith of their fathers, but they deeply missed the temple.

Nehemiah and Ezra began the rebuilding campaign in the fifth century BC. The temple was begun in 537 BC and completed in 515 BC. The city walls were finished later in 445 BC. The Samaritans and other neighbors of Judah opposed this process. The Samaritans historically lived in northern Palestine. During the Babylonian exile, many of the Samaritans migrated into Jerusalem and Judah, taking over the vacated houses and farms of the Jews. When the Jews returned, they wanted their family property returned. This created tremendous friction between the Samaritans and Jews. The Jews already despised the Samaritans. They considered them half-breeds, a mixture of Assyrian blood and Jewish blood that occurred during the Assyrian domination of Israel (2 Kings 17).

The Samaritans worshipped Yahweh as the God of the land—he gave fertility to the soil. They followed the Pentateuch (the five books of Moses), but they rejected the prophetic books and the books of poetry in the Jewish canon. They built a sanctuary on Mount Gerizim. Later, during the reign of Alexander the Great, they built a temple upon it.[6] The Samaritans proudly pointed out to the Jews that Jerusalem was never mentioned in the Pentateuch, but their holy place—Mount Gerizim—was (Deuteronomy 11:29, 27:12-13).

The bitterness between these two races broke into warfare in 128 BC. The Jews, led by John Hyrcanus, marched into Samaria and destroyed the temple on Mount Gerizim. Even though the temple was never rebuilt, the Samaritans held onto the belief that Mount Gerizim was their holy place. The animosity between the Jews and Samaritans continued through New Testament times. But we will learn more about those times leading up to the first century in our next chapter.

Notes

1. Compare Matthew 2:15 with Hosea 11:1-2; Matthew 21:5 and Isaiah 62:11 with Zechariah 9:9; and Matthew 27:2-10 with Zechariah 11:12-13. In Paul's writings compare Ephesians 4:8 with Psalm 68:18, 1 Corinthians 10:4 with Exodus 17:6 and Numbers 20:11. Compare also Hebrews 1:5 with 2 Samuel 7:12-15 and Psalm 2:7.

2. Many premillennialists ignore NT usage of OT prophecies in order to make the Old Testament fit their system.

3. The date of the Exodus is perhaps the one most debated topic in OT chronology. Some conservative scholars, on the basis of such passages as 1 Kings 6:1,

Judges 11:26 and Acts 13:17-20, contend that the Exodus must be dated about 1445 BC. Others believe these passages can be harmonized with a date around 1290 BC, which they feel is supported by other Biblical data and is necessitated by certain archaeological evidence.

4. Gleason L. Archer, *A Survey of Old Testament Introduction* (Grand Rapids: Zondervan, 1982), 262.

5. The law of Levirate marriage was established in Genesis 38 and Deuteronomy 25:5-10. When a man died without leaving a son, his widow was not to marry outside the family. The husband's brother was to marry her. If he was not willing, then someone in his family line was to marry her. If no one could be found to marry her, then a ceremony was performed that freed her to marry outside the family.

6. Recent archaeological digs have discovered this temple. It is believed to have been modeled after the temple of Jerusalem; therefore, a view of this temple might give us a glimpse of what the temple of Jerusalem looked like.

9

The Intertestamental Period

If Malachi was the last book written in the Old Testament, we have more than 400 years of history during which no books in our Bible were written. However, the events during those years are extremely important for those wanting to understand the fears, expectations and hopes we find among the Jewish people when Jesus came.

Palestine Under the Greeks

The Persians, until the Battle of Issus in 333 BC, controlled Palestine. At this battle Alexander the Great, a young Greek ruler, conquered the Persian King Darius III. The Macedonians marched through Palestine to wage war against Egypt. The Jews surrendered to Alexander's troops without battle. The Greeks allowed the Jews the same freedoms afforded them by the Persians.

The rise of Hellenistic (from *hellene* = Greek) culture marks the beginning of Western civilization. The Greeks strongly exerted their influence on neighboring cultures. They did not need to enforce Greek ways—because of their success, people desired to be like them. The Greek culture strongly influenced Palestine, and its influence can be seen in the fact that the New Testament was written in *Koine* Greek, the Greek used in everyday life. The Phoenicians and Philistines became so enamored by the Greeks that they exchanged their language for Greek, and the distinctive aspects of their culture were lost.

The Jews also felt the sway of Hellenism, but not as strongly as their neighbors did. From the Greeks they learned to debate and use didactic conversation when attempting to clarify the divine will. They did not fully embrace the Greeks, and they certainly did not accept the Greek gods.

In 323 BC, at the age of thirty-three, Alexander the Great suddenly died. The empire he left behind was vast. His death threw the empire into confusion. The Greek governor of Egypt, Ptolemy, and the Greek governor of Syria, Antigonus, waged war for control of Palestine. Eventually, Ptolemy won and Egypt, a Hellenistic state, controlled Palestine for more than one hundred years, from 312-198 BC. The governors of Palestine during this time were known as the Ptolemies. The Ptolemies allowed the Jews to be led by the high priests and the Sanhedrin—the priests, scribes and elders. The power of the high priests and the Sanhedrin, which is witnessed in the New Testament, descended from this period.

The Seleucids were the Syrian governors who controlled the territory north of Palestine. After the reign of the Ptolemies, the Seleucids controlled Palestine from 198-143 BC. At the beginning of the second century BC, Antiochus III (the Great) wrested control of Palestine from Egypt. Once in control, the Seleucids continued the policies of the Ptolemies, allowing the high priests to control Palestine.

In 175 BC Antiochus IV (Epiphanes) began to rule in Syria. Epiphanes means "the manifest god," and the Jews made a play on this word, calling the ruler "Antiochus Epimanes," meaning "the insane." At this time Onias, a devout observer of the law, was high priest. Onias' brother, Joshua, wedded himself to the Greek and Hellenization, changed his name to Jason and opposed his brother. Jason convinced Antiochus IV to strip Onias of the high priesthood and give it to him. Thus Jason became high priest and began an intense Hellenization campaign across Jerusalem. He built a gymnasium in Jerusalem where the participants would compete naked, as was the Greek tradition. During these games the Greeks would make fun of the Jews who had been circumcised. Many of the Jewish participants, including some priests, tried to have their circumcision surgically reversed in order to escape ridicule (1 Maccabees 1:15).

Later, a Jew named Menelaus offered the Syrian governor a higher bribe for the high priesthood. Thus, Menelaus replaced Jason as high priest, and the office became open to the highest bidder.

In 169 BC Antiochus IV entered Jerusalem to replenish his own treasury, which had been depleted from battles with Egypt and Rome. He plundered the Jerusalem temple, taking with him the altar of incense, the seven-branched lampstand and the table of shewbread (1 Maccabees 1:20-24).

A short time later the Syrians and Antiochus IV entered Jerusalem with the purpose of enforcing Hellenization upon the Jews. They decided to destroy the Jewish communities and their indigenous way of life. They tore down the walls of Jerusalem, built a fortress on the hill of the ancient city of David (the Acra), forbid the Jews on the pain of death to keep the Sabbath or to circumcise their children, erected a pagan altar on the site of the altar of burnt offerings and offered a pig upon the altar of Yahweh as a sacrifice to their supreme god, Olympia Zeus (167 BC).

This act became known as the "abomination that causes desolation" that was spoken of by the prophet Daniel (11:31, 12:11). Jesus refers to this event in Mark's gospel and indicates that another occurrence like it will be one of the signs that would surround the destruction of the temple in Jerusalem (Mark 13:15). The event is also described in 1 Maccabees 1:54-64:

> Now on the fifteenth day of Chislev, in the one hundred and forty-fifth year, they erected a desolating sacrilege upon the altar of burnt offering. They also built altars in the surrounding cities of Judah, and burned incense at the doors of the houses and in the streets. The books of the law which they found they tore to pieces and burned with fire. Where the book of the covenant was found in the possession of any one, or if any one adhered to the law, the decree of the king condemned him to death. They kept using violence against Israel, against those found month after month in the cities. And on the twenty-fifth day of the month they offered sacrifice on the altar which was upon the altar of burnt offering. According to the decree, they put to death the women who had their children circumcised, and their families and those who circumcised them; and they hung the infants from their mothers' necks. But many in Israel stood firm and were resolved in their hearts not to eat unclean food. They chose to die rather than to be defiled by food or to profane the holy covenant; and they did die. And very great wrath came upon Israel.

Pious Jews died rather than submit to the whims of Antiochus IV. The Jews in the countryside outside of Jerusalem were especially antagonistic toward the Syrians. Some of these rebels banned together under the leadership of an old priest named Mattathias. This led to what is known as the Maccabean revolt.

The Maccabean Revolt

The cruelty and harshness of the Seleucid rulers (especially Antiochus IV) led many of the Jews of Palestine to openly rebel. The seeds of this revolution began in the countryside in a small village named Modein. The Syrians came to this village to compel the Jews to offer pagan sacrifices. An old priest named Mattathias from the Hasmonean family, killed the Jew who was going to make the sacrifice and the royal officer who ordered it. Thus began the revolt.

The revolt progressed under the leadership of Mattathias' oldest son, Judas Maccabeus. Judas was given the nickname "the Maccabean," which means "hammer-like." (The history of the Maccabean revolt is recorded in the Apocrypha in 1 and 2 Maccabees.) Feeling the pressure of the rebel forces, Antiochus sent his commander, Lysias, to crush the revolt. Judas brilliantly practiced the art of guerilla warfare and over a period of two years was able to defeat Antiochus' much larger forces.

On the twenty-fifth of *Kislev* (roughly corresponding to our December) in the year 164 BC, the altar of Yahweh was consecrated anew and an eight-day feast was celebrated. This became the Feast of Dedication or Hanukkah. During this celebration lamps are lit to show that shadows and darkness must always give way to light—the Festival of Lights.

When Antiochus IV died, the Syrian kingdom was thrown into turmoil. To ease the tension in Palestine, Lysias allowed the Jews to resume their normal spiritual life and the rituals of the temple. Judas and his followers had won a victory. More importantly for students of the Bible, Judas and his brothers influenced the way Jews would think about the kind of messiah God would send to rescue his people. When Jesus came, many would be disappointed that he did not lead like the Maccabean.

Through these events, the Jews were left without a high priest. The Syrians placed Alkimus in this position. Alkimus was a friend of Hellenization and also a descendent of the Aaronic family. Many of the Jews eagerly accepted Alkimus as high priest. Judas Maccabeus and his family, however, rejected him. Yet Judas died in 160 BC without doing anything about this situation.

However, his brother Jonathan did do something. He took over leadership of the Maccabean rebels after Judas died. In 153 BC Jonathan persuaded the Syrians to allow him to become high priest. Jonathan, stained by the blood of war and not of the priestly family, assumed the role of high priest until he was killed in 143 BC.

After Jonathan, Simon, the last surviving son of Mattathias, assumed the role of high priest. He was a military commander. In 140 BC he took office as high priest, field commander and leader of the Jews. This began a hereditary dynasty, which would become known as the Hasmonean dynasty. The Romans would eventually accept the leadership of the Hasmoneans, at least for a time.

Simon's rule was praised as being a time of peace and happiness—1 Maccabees 14:8-15 records:

> They tilled their land in peace; the ground gave its increase, and the trees of the plains their fruit. Old men sat in the streets; they all talked together of good things; and the youths donned the glories and garments of war. He supplied the cities with food, and furnished them with the means of defense, till his renown spread to the ends of the earth. He established peace in the land, and Israel rejoiced with great joy. Each man sat under his vine and his fig tree, and there was none to make them afraid. No one was left in the land to fight them, and the kings were crushed in those days. He strengthened all the humble of his people; he sought out the law, and did away with every lawless and wicked man. He made the sanctuary glorious, and added to the vessels of the sanctuary.

Many devout Jews disapproved of the Hasmoneans since they took the title of high priests, but were not of the line of Aaron—and rulers, but were not of the house of David. Some left Jerusalem and started communities around the Dead Sea that were centered on a strict following of the law. One of these communities was Qumran—home of the Essenes and the Dead Sea Scrolls. Simon's rule ended when he was murdered in 134 BC by a son-in-law of Ptolemy.

The Hasmonean Kingdom

In 134 BC John Hyrcanus took control of Palestine after the death of his father, Simon. Simon had set himself up as ruler, high priest and military commander. John Hyrcanus inherited this title for himself. He began a series of military campaigns that would secure Palestine. In 128 BC he defeated the Syrians and pushed them out of Palestine. Also, in that same year, he destroyed the Samaritan temple on Mount Gerizim. Although he was popular with many Jews, the Pharisees (those more concerned with Jewish purity) rejected him. He simply made new alliances with the Sadducees (the more aristocratic and pragmatically minded sect, more open to Greek influences, and more focused on worldly power).

Aristobulus, the son of John Hyrcanus, took the rule after the death of his father. He became the first Jewish ruler since the exile to wear the title "king."

Significant to New Testament students is the fact that Aristobulus conquered Galilee and forced many non-Jews to become proselytes. Since Jesus chose his disciples in Galilee, it is likely that some of them were from Greek families that had been proselyted into Judaism. This background helps us understand some of slurs about Galileans that one would have heard in Jerusalem because of their suspect Jewish heritage.

Aristobulus was succeeded by his brother Alexander Jannaeus. His real name was Jonathan. When he became king, he took on a Greek name to strengthen his influence with the non-Jews. He continued the military campaigns of John Hyrcanus. He increased the borders of the kingdom to a size approximate to that of Solomon's kingdom. He forced his conquered territories to become Jewish, which caused constant revolt in these territories.

Alexander Jannaeus was a man of war, and yet he held the office of high priest. The Pharisees rejected him because of this. Jannaeus responded by capturing eight hundred of the offenders. He had a banquet prepared for their wives and children. Then he had these men crucified as their families watched. This was the first time crucifixion was used in Judea—a Jew used it on Jews—but not the last. Alexander Jannaeus was a harsh ruler who ruled with terror. Although people feared him, they did not respect him.

After Alexander Jannaeus' death, his wife, Salome Alexandra, ruled the kingdom. The brothers of Jannaeus, Hyrcanus II and Aristobulus II, fought for control of Judea. All of these disputes were overshadowed by the rise to power of the mighty Roman Empire. Around 63 BC, Pompey, a commander of the Roman army, entered Jerusalem and went into the temple, even inspecting the Holy of Holies. Palestine was now in Roman hands.

Palestine Under Roman Rule

In 64-63 BC Pompey entered Syria and Palestine. After a three-month siege, Pompey conquered Jerusalem. Pompey began to shape Palestine after Roman rule and order. He gave Palestine the texture that we read about in the New Testament. He took the ruler, Aristobulus II, back to Rome as a prisoner. He installed Hyrcanus II as high priest, and he redrew the boundaries of Palestine, dividing the lands that Alexander Jannaeus conquered. He set up a free league of cities in the east ranging from Damascus in the north to Philadelphia in the south—known as the Decapolis. He freed Samaria. The high priest now only controlled Jerusalem, Judea and the interior of Galilee and Perea.

Later, in 57 BC, the Roman provincial governor of Syria, Gabinius, divided Palestine into five districts, which remained the same for many years:

- Judea: Jerusalem, Gazara, Jericho
- Galilee: Sepphoris
- Perea: Amanthus

In Rome, Pompey and Caesar began to squabble over control of the Empire. Pompey was murdered in Egypt in 48 BC, and Caesar took control. Hyrcanus II quickly drew the favor of Caesar, who kept him as high priest in Jerusalem. Antipater was installed as the procurator of Judea. Now a high priest and a Roman governor whose allegiances were first to Rome governed Judea. Antipater shared his power with his two sons Phasael, administrator of Judea, and Herod, administrator of Galilee.

In 44 BC Caesar was murdered, and confusion broke out across the Empire. Octavian and Antony gained control of Rome from those who killed Caesar in the battle at Philippi. Antony took control of the Eastern empire and lived with the Egyptian queen Cleopatra in Alexandria. Antony allowed Hyrcanus II to remain as high priest. Antipater, however, was murdered. The rule of Palestine fell into the hands of his sons Phasael and Herod.

In 40 BC Antigonus, who would be the last hope of the Hasmonean dynasty and the son of Aristobulus II, who was captured earlier by Pompey, came with the Parthians from the east and gained power over Judea. Phasael, the governor of Judea, rather than be captured, killed himself. Antigonus mutilated his uncle, the high priest, Hyrcanus, so that he could never be high priest again. Antigonus then set himself up as ruler and high priest from 40-37 BC.

At this time Herod, the governor of Galilee, traveled to Rome and asked for help of Octavian and Anthony. In 40 BC the Senate named Herod "the king of the Jews" but he was a king without a country until 37 BC when the Romans conquered Palestine and Herod took his seat as "king of the Jews" (a position he would jealously guard). Antigonus was executed. He would be but one of many to die under Herod's rule.

10

New Testament Times

Jesus was born in now famously humble circumstances. He grew up in a tiny and obscure village, but all around him was a society in turmoil. (See figure 6 for an outline of the rulers of Palestine from the accession of Herod the Great to the beginning of the Judeo-Roman War.) Political and religious tensions were high. Palestine in the first century was anything but serene.

Herod the Great

In Rome, Octavian defeated Pompey for control of the Roman Empire. Octavian gave himself a new name—Caesar Augustus. In Palestine, Herod, whose Jewish lineage was greatly suspect, was purging the land of all of his opponents. He married Mariamne, who was of the lineage of the Hasmoneans. This gave him the appearance of continuing the Hasmonean dynasty.

Herod, however, never felt secure. After murdering old Hyrcanus II, he gave the high priesthood to his brother-in-law, Aristobulus. Herod realized his error—he had given the priesthood to a descendant of the Hasmoneans. Within a year, he had Aristobulus murdered in his bath. Later he killed his wife, Mariamne, and their two sons, Alexander and Aristobulus, for fear of their Hasmonean blood. The New Testament accounts which describe the murder of infant boys two years and younger for fear that one was a future king (Matthew 2:16) is in line with the historical testimony of the character of Herod the Great.

Herod ruled both Judea and Galilee. He was over both Jews and Gentiles. He wanted to be considered as a Jew to the Jews and as a Gentile to the Gentiles. For the Gentiles he rebuilt their cities, adding gymnasiums, theaters and pagan temples. For the Jews he rebuilt their temple and enlarged it, giving it the form it had in Solomon's day. This temple became known as

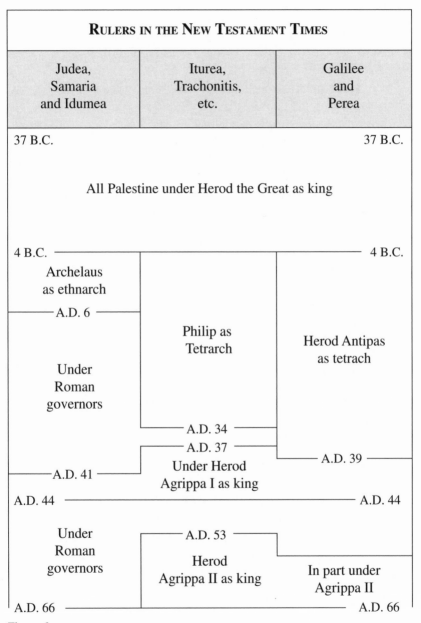

RULERS IN THE NEW TESTAMENT TIMES		
Judea, Samaria and Idumea	Iturea, Trachonitis, etc.	Galilee and Perea

37 B.C.   37 B.C.

All Palestine under Herod the Great as king

4 B.C. ─────────────────────────── 4 B.C.

Archelaus as ethnarch

── A.D. 6 ──

Philip as Tetrarch

Herod Antipas as tetrach

Under Roman governors

── A.D. 34 ──
── A.D. 37 ──
Under Herod Agrippa I as king

── A.D. 39 ──

── A.D. 41 ──

A.D. 44 ─────────────────────────── A.D. 44

Under Roman governors

── A.D. 53 ──
Herod Agrippa II as king

In part under Agrippa II

A.D. 66 ─────────────────────────── A.D. 66

Figure 6

Herod's temple. It was destroyed by the Romans in 70 AD, and today, all that remains of Herod's temple is the famous Wailing Wall in Jerusalem. In spite of the rebuilding of the temple, many Jews hated Herod. He was a ruthless tyrant, a friend of Romans and pagans.

Herod accomplished much during his reign. He built Sebaste on the site of the destroyed city of Samaria. He built Caesarea on the coast. He constructed Antonia, a strong citadel in Jerusalem, which looked down upon the temple court. He built Masada on the top of a mountain by the Dead Sea. Masada was a great fortress that later became the spot of a tremendous standoff between the Romans and the Jews and a symbol of Jewish perseverance and determination.

During Herod's reign, both Jesus and John the Baptist were born. When Herod died, his kingdom was divided into three parts, ruled at first by three sons who had amazingly survived his murderous jealousy.

- Archelaus: Judea, Samaria, Idumea
- Herod Antipas: Galilee and Perea
- Phillip: the Transjordan (area northeast of the Jordan)

Herod's Progeny
Archelaus

Of the three sons of Herod the Great, the most hated was Archelaus, and his reign would be the most brief. In AD 6 a petition was sent to Augustus in Rome asking for the removal of Archelaus. The Romans agreed with the populace and exiled him to Gaul, replacing him with a Roman governor. Thus, in the time of Jesus, Roman procurators (governors) ruled over Judea, Samaria and Idumea (Luke 3:1). The first governor adopted a lenient policy toward the Jews, allowing them to keep their religious ceremonies without interference from Rome. The governor allowed the Sanhedrin to rule over the Jewish populace, but they could not inflict the death penalty.

In Jesus' day Pontius Pilate was the Roman governor over Judea. Philo of Alexandria noted that Pilate's office was known for corruption, violence, depredations, ill treatment, offenses, numerous illegal executions and incessant, unbearable cruelty. Pilate cared little for the religious sensitivities of the Jews, openly displaying pictures of the Emperor in Jerusalem. He also took money from the temple treasury to build an aqueduct into Jerusalem. The New Testament testimony confirms this harsh picture of Pilate. He would have easily complied with the Jewish leaders to execute an innocent man on the charges of sedition. Thus, Jesus of Nazareth was killed outside the gates of Jerusalem, suffering the most intense, shameful punishment devised by man.

Herod Antipas

In the north in Galilee, Herod Antipas ruled from 4 BC to AD 39. He built a palace on a cemetery and named it Tiberias after the reigning emperor. None of the Jews around him would live there because they considered it unclean. His first wife was a daughter of the Nabataean king. Later he took Herodias (the wife of his half brother) as his wife. He sent his first wife back to her father. His marriage to Herodias would haunt him throughout his reign. Not only did he run into conflict with John the Baptist over it, but the Nabataean king was also highly offended by the return of his daughter. He attacked Galilee and handed Herod Antipas a sound defeat. Many saw this defeat as retribution from God for the way Antipas treated John the Baptist.

Since Herod Antipas was in control of Galilee, and most of Jesus' ministry was in Galilee, Herod was ruler over Jesus' homeland. Herod's first exposure to Jesus was startling in that he thought that Jesus was John the Baptist returned from the dead (Luke 9:7-9). Herod Antipas met Jesus just before the Crucifixion. Pilate sent Jesus to Herod so that Antipas might pass judgment upon him (Luke 23:6-16). Antipas declined to pass sentence and returned Jesus to Pilate.

In the end Herodias was Antipas' undoing. She persuaded him to press Caligula for the title "King of Galilee." Caligula rejected the title and chose instead to exile Herod Antipas to Gaul in AD 39.

Philip

In the northern Transjordan, Philip was the ruler. He built a new city, which he named Caesarea Philippi. Jesus went there only once that we know of. Philip was the first Jewish ruler to mint a coin bearing his image. He died in AD 34, leaving behind no heir.

Herod Agrippa

In Acts 12 we are introduced to Herod Agrippa, the grandson of Herod the Great. In AD 37 Caligula first gave Agrippa the territory Philip had controlled, and two years later, he exiled Herod Antipas and gave Agrippa his territory. In AD 41 Judea, Samaria and Idumea were added to his control. Thus, for a brief time under Agrippa the territory that Herod the Great had once ruled was reunited. During his reign, Caligula threatened to have his image placed in the temple of Jerusalem. This failed to happen because in AD 41 Caligula was murdered. In his place Claudius became Caesar. Agrippa was like his grandfather Herod in that he attempted to be a Jew to the Jews and a Gentile to the Gentiles. For the Greeks he built buildings. For the Jews he persecuted Christians. He had James beheaded and Peter thrown in jail. After Agrippa, Roman governors once again took control of Judea and Galilee.

Agrippa II

The last member of Herod's family to lead in Palestine was Agrippa's son. He was a minor in Rome when his father died, but he later returned to govern portions of Galilee and Judea. In this role, he was also allowed to control the temple. The pious Jews resented him because he gave the high priesthood to whomever he wished. They were also offended because he kept his sister, Bernice, close to him at all times. Rumors spread that they were in an incestuous relationship. We first find Agrippa in the New Testament in Acts 25 when Paul appears before him.

When there was no member of Herod's family providing leadership in some part of Palestine, the Romans sent in governors. In AD 52 Felix became governor of Judea. When Paul was imprisoned in Caesarea, he made his defense before Felix. In AD 60 Porcius Festus became governor of Judea. He died in AD 62.

During the reign of these Roman governors, the Jews became restless. Many of them wanted to see their land rid of the Romans once and for all. Some were even willing to fight to see this goal realized. This led to the Jewish War of the AD 60s.

The Jewish War

Palestine entered turbulent years during AD 60-70. The Jews' hatred for the occupying forces of the Romans increased. Tension mounted and then war erupted. The spark that ignited this was the action of a Roman governor, Gessius Florus. He was so greedy that he sent people into the temple treasury to steal just seventeen talents (AD 66). The Jews responded by going through Jerusalem begging alms for poor Gessius Florus. The governor became enraged and allowed the Roman soldiers to plunder the city. When Florus sent two more cohorts into the city, rebels united and drove the Romans out. Only one cohort remained, and they were held up in the citadel of Antonia. The rebel's success spurred others to join their ranks. The fires of war were now raging.

The Romans countered by sending Cestius, the Syrian governor, and his troops into Judea. Cestius could not take Jerusalem, however, and he was sent back home in defeat. The Jews celebrated their newly won liberty and buckled down for the next assault by Rome.

Nero had become Caesar of Rome. He gave his best general, Vespasian, charge of the war against the Jews. Vespasian took his son, Titus, with him to wage this war in the east.

A young priest named Josephus joined the Jewish rebels in their campaign against Rome. When Vespasian marched into Galilee, Josephus entrenched himself in Jotapata with other rebels. They held off the Romans for forty-seven days. When their defeat was imminent, the Zealots urged everyone to commit suicide. Josephus decided to place his future with the Romans. He surrendered to Vespasian and praised the general, telling him he would be the next Caesar. Vespasian decided to spare Josephus, and he kept him in his military headquarters. He eventually lived in Rome under imperial patronage, and it was from there that he wrote his well-known historical works including *The Jewish War.*

By AD 67, all of Galilee was again in Roman hands. Rome next turned her eyes toward Jerusalem. In the city of Jerusalem radical groups had taken over. They waged battles against each other for control of the city while the populace watched in fear. The Christian community, being warned of the impending doom of the city through the prophecies of Jesus, fled Jerusalem and headed toward Pella beyond the Jordan. In AD 69 Vespasian became Emperor of Rome. His son, Titus, carried on the war in Jerusalem.

During the Passover of AD 70, Titus marched on Jerusalem. Because of the holiday season, it was swollen in size. Titus laid siege to the city. Jewish resistance fighters were nailed to crosses on the banks outside the city in order to intimidate those who remained inside. The intensity of the Zealots held strong, but the Romans were stronger.

The Romans pushed into the city and set fire to the temple. Titus entered the Holy of Holies just in time to seize the seven-branched lampstand and the table of shewbread. They marched these emblems back to Rome as trophies of war. The temple was left in ruins. The most holy symbol of Judaism had now been destroyed.

After the destruction of the temple, Titus initiated two actions. First, he deported as many Jews as possible back to Rome as slaves. Second, he renamed the land—*Palaestima*—Land of the Philistines. The Jews despised this name because they despised the Philistines.

Even though the temple had been lost, some Jewish resistance fighters still held hope for victory. These small bands of warriors were scattered throughout Judea. The strongest enclave was entrenched in the fortress of Herod the Great—Masada. Masada was built high upon a plateau in Judea. A path called "the snake path" was the only way into the fortress. Its location made access to it extremely difficult. The Roman governor, Flavius Silva, spent three years building an assault ramp, which extended three hundred feet into the air.

In the spring of AD 74 the Romans were finally ready to enter the fortress. The Zealots inside Masada ordered mass suicide rather than be captured by the Romans. The men took the lives of their own families. Ten men were chosen to kill the rest, and then one was chosen to kill the last ten. Upon entering the fortress the Romans found everyone dead except two women and five children who had hidden in the water tunnels of the fortress. The Jews had burned everything except their food. They wanted the Romans to know that they did not starve.

During the destruction of Jerusalem, the Sadducees were executed. The Pharisees, most of whom fled to the city of Jamnia, took it upon themselves to keep the traditions of Judaism alive. They heightened the influence of community synagogues. While Judaism survived the fall of Jerusalem, it was never the same after the destruction of the temple. The ultraorthodox Jewish sects today still long for it to be rebuilt.

11

The Gospels and Acts

In the Ptolemaic period, the word "gospel" was used when a king was born and especially when he ascended the throne. It means "good news," the report by the herald of a king. The message of this was *euangellion*, the gospel. Even earlier, it meant the fee paid to a messenger who brought good news to a general in battle. The Christians adopted this word and applied it to Jesus, who was their king. They were announcing his ascension to the throne of God.

The early Christians also added to it the Jewish concept of the living word. For the Jew, the Word was never just a report or a story—it was always the living and active word of God (Hebrews 4:12).

In the New Testament, the "gospel" came to mean the living word of preaching Christ as King." This is how Mark uses the term as he opens his gospel in Mark 1:1, "The beginning of the gospel about Jesus Christ." This is not just a nice story or a common book that he is writing. He is heralding the coming and ascension of the King of the universe. The Gospel writers are not dispassionate journalists or historians reporting on Jesus. They are believers who write to promote faith in this man whom they knew to be like no other (Luke 1:1-4, John 20:31).

The Synoptic Gospels

The first three gospels are often referred to as the "synoptic" Gospels. "Synoptic" means "with a common eye or common view." Matthew, Mark and Luke all cover the same basic material in the life of Jesus. However, they each have their distinctive characteristics.

Philosophical Background of the New Testament

Platonism—This system was dualistic. Plato said that two worlds existed—one was this world; the other was the ideal world. Everything in this world has its ideal match in the other world—the real world. The goal of life is to get free enough from this world to see into the real world. Death brings victory because the soul escapes the prison house of the body and is free to see all the good of the real world.

Epicureanism—"Whatever brings you happiness is truth." Epicurus advocated the intelligent pursuit of pleasure.

Stoicism—It is called "stoicism" because Zeno, the founder of this school, taught under a porch, *stoa* in Greek. Stoics believed everything was controlled by the divine logos or divine reason (fate). The best way to live was to learn to passively accept whatever life might bring. Stoicism stressed the need to rid oneself of emotions and desires.

Cynicism—*Cynic* means "like a dog." Just as a dog is part of the natural order, we are part of the natural order. This was the back-to-nature movement of the ancient world. The best life was the simple life and the cynics rejected the need for all extravagance. The distinct form of presentation used by their wandering teachers was the "diatribe" in which the speaker would first ask a question and then answer it. Paul uses something similar to this in Romans 6.

Mark

Authorship

Although none of the gospel writers gives his name, there is evidence for the authors whose names came to be attached to the documents. John Mark, a disciple of Peter, wrote the gospel of Mark. Irenaeus, an early church leader who died around AD 200, wrote that after the death of Peter and Paul in AD 64-65, Mark, the associate of Peter, handed down the preaching of Peter in the gospel of Mark. Another early church leader, Papias (c. 115), was quoted by church historian Eusebius as saying,

> ...and John the Presbyter also said this—"Mark, being the interpreter of Peter, whatsoever he recorded he wrote with great accuracy, but not,

however, in the order in which it was spoken or done by our Lord, for he neither heard nor followed our Lord, but as before said, he was in company with Peter, who gave him such instruction as was necessary, but not to give a history of our Lord's discourses: wherefore Mark has not erred in anything, by writing some things as he has recorded them; for he was carefully attentive to one thing, not to pass by anything he heard, or to state anything falsely in these accounts."

New Testament scholar Merrill Tenney summarizes,

"From these considerations it may be concluded that this Gospel is the product of one of the junior preachers of the apostolic age, who was thoroughly acquainted with the message concerning Jesus and who recorded it as he heard it, without elaboration or embellishments of any kind. He made no attempt at a biographical interpretation; he merely allowed the facts themselves to speak for him."[1]

Date and Place of Writing

Mark was probably written in Rome (or perhaps to the Christians in Rome) during the time of the persecutions of Nero. This is supported by the early church father, Clement of Alexandra. Nero executed both Paul and Peter around the year 65. Between 63-70, the Christians in Rome faced severe persecution. More than half of Mark's gospel contains material about Jesus facing the cross. This theme would have strengthened those facing persecution from Nero.

Most scholars date the gospel between 65 and 70. This would be some time after the death of Peter and before the destruction of Jerusalem.

Audience

Mark wrote to the Gentile Christians in Rome. New Testament scholar F. F. Bruce states,

The life-setting in which this Gospel was published was probably the Emperor Nero's attack on the Christians of Rome in the months following the devastation of that city by fire in AD 64. Shaken and nearly demoralized by the suddenness and ferocity of this attack, they sorely needed to be reassured of the validity of their faith.... If they had to suffer for Christ's sake, they were but following in the steps of their Lord, who himself had suffered at the hands of the Roman power.[2]

This setting matches the theme of Mark's gospel—the theme of discipleship to Christ.

Purpose

Mark wrote to explain to the Gentile world the nature of Jesus. He was correcting the Hellenistic "divine man" image of Jesus. In Mark 1:1-8:26, he portrays Jesus as miracle worker. In Mark 8:27-16:8, he pictures Jesus as the suffering Son of Man.

Mark's gospel also serves as a guide to strengthen fellow Christians who are undergoing persecution. In the same way that Jesus went to the cross, his followers must take up their crosses and follow him. In the first century, the cross only had one meaning: death. The disciples of Jesus had to be ready to die for their faith.

Characteristics

Mark's style is energetic, brisk and full of action. He uses the historical present (the present tense used as past action) 151 times. Mark uses the word "and" often. In the Greek of chapter 3, twenty-nine out of the thirty-five verses begin with the word "and." He uses the word "immediately" some forty-one times in his gospel. Jesus "gallops" from one place to the next, doing the work of God.

Mark's is a very Gentile-oriented gospel. He does not use many Jewish terms, and when he does, he explains them to his Greek audience.

Luke

Authorship

Luke was a traveling companion of Paul, referred to in Paul's letters. The "we" sections in Acts are a travel diary of Luke with Paul (Acts 16:10-17, 20:5-15, 21:1-18, 27:1-28:16). Luke was a physician and a historian. His prologue in Luke 1:1-4 describes how he wrote his gospel. Merrill Tenney believes that Luke was an Antiochian Gentile who accompanied Paul on his second journey. Luke remained an evangelist in Philippi, then he accompanied Paul on his third journey. Colossians mentions that he was not a Jew (Colossians 4:10-14). This makes Luke the only non-Jewish writer of the New Testament. Eusebius says that Luke was from Antioch in Syria. Tenney writes,

> Accordingly, the author of Luke-Acts may have been an Antiochian Gentile, converted in Antioch not more than fifteen years after Pentecost. He became

a friend and associate of Paul and traveled with him on the second journey after meeting him at Troas (Acts 16:10). He remained at Philippi as evangelist of the church while Paul pursued his itinerant ministry in Achaia and visited Antioch in Asia Minor (18:22, 19:1-41). When Paul returned to Philippi on the third journey, the author again joined his company (20:6). He went with him to the mainland of Asia, and then accompanied him to Jerusalem.[3]

Date and Place of Writing

Luke was likely written shortly after Mark's gospel. He could have written it around 67-68. Some scholars would date it earlier, c. 57-60 (many would say around AD 64). Tenney states,

> It must have been written before Acts.... Acts was probably composed prior to the close of Paul's first imprisonment at Rome, since the abrupt ending of the book intimates that the author had no more to say.... Perhaps AD 60 would serve as a median date, for by that time Luke would have been a Christian at least ten years or more, and would have traveled in Palestine, where he could have met many of those who had known Jesus in the flesh.[4]

The place of writing is unknown. It would certainly seem that it was written somewhere outside of Palestine.

Audience

Luke's audience is almost certainly Gentile. Luke was a Gentile writer, writing to a Gentile audience. He was a well-educated and careful writer with an excellent command of the Greek language.

Purpose

In Luke 1:1-4, he states that his purpose was to write an orderly account of what happened in the life and ministry of Jesus. Luke was attempting to attract and win cultured citizens in the Gentile world. He gave a picture of God's saving work in the world. He was writing a form of "salvation history." He gave his audience (*Theophilus* is "lover of God") enough material to decide whether he wanted to be a Christian.

Characteristics

When placed alongside Acts, Luke's gospel gives a comprehensive history of the ministry of Jesus and the early church. His writings are the longest in the New Testament, making up twenty-seven percent of the NT material.

Luke's gospel especially includes the stories that show Jesus' commit-ment to the poor, the less fortunate and the oppressed. Luke highlights Jesus' different attitude toward Samaritans, women and others often excluded from society.

Luke includes the theme of prayer often in his work. He also has more references to the Holy Spirit than Matthew and Mark combined.

Luke uses sixty percent of Mark's material, which makes up forty percent of his gospel. Twenty percent of Luke comes from a source that is common with Matthew. The other thirty-eight percent is found only in Luke. He writes like a historian. No other gospel writer gives us historical references like Luke. The gospel is very literate, being the most readable of the Gospels. His vocabulary is rich and varied.

Matthew

Authorship

The apostle Matthew wrote the gospel of Matthew. In AD 130, Papius wrote, "Matthew composed the *logia* in the Hebrew tongue." Irenaeus stated that Matthew composed his gospel in Hebrew. He states, "Matthew also issued a written gospel among the Hebrews in their own dialect, while Peter and Paul were preaching at Rome and laying the foundations of the church." The early church leader, Ignatius of Antioch, quotes only Matthew. For this reason, many scholars believe it was written from Antioch.

Matthew was also known as Levi. He was a tax collector whom Jesus called to be an apostle (Matthew 9:9-13, 10:3). After he is listed in Acts 1:13, we know nothing more of him.

Date and Place of Writing

Most scholars date Matthew's gospel between 80-85. They place it after the temple was destroyed and after Mark's gospel. Most scholars date it after Luke. But there is no reason to date it this late. It could have been written at the same time as Luke's gospel—around AD 67-68. It should be placed somewhere between 50 and 70.

The traditional place of writing is Palestine. Matthew's gospel seems to be written for a Jewish audience. But it could have been written to Jews outside of Palestine. Two NT scholars, B. H. Streeter and Merrill Tenney, believe that it was written in Antioch of Syria. Tenney writes,

The place of writing could be Antioch....This first Gospel was probably the favorite of the Syro-Jewish church. Furthermore, the church at Antioch was the first to have a markedly Gentile constituency that spoke Aramaic and Greek.... It may, therefore, have been composed some time between AD 50 and 70 and have been circulated by those who worked in and from the church of Antioch.[5]

Audience

Matthew was writing to Jewish Christians in the second half of the first century. His is the only gospel with a distinctive Jewish orientation. It contains approximately forty fulfillment citations. Matthew uses several Hebrew phrases that he does not bother to translate. He normally uses the phrase "kingdom of heaven" (which would have been more common among a Jewish audience) rather than "kingdom of God."

Purpose

Matthew's gospel is apologetic in nature, meaning that it is written as a defense. He was writing to convince Jewish readers that Jesus was the Messiah—the son of the living God. The birth/infancy narratives defend the birth of Jesus as miraculous and legitimate. In his resurrection account he includes the bribery of the guards to demonstrate that Jesus' body was not stolen.

Matthew also wants to show that the church is the true Israel. Jesus came to fulfill the law of Moses. In doing so, he ushered in a new kingdom, a spiritual kingdom. Matthew attempts to show the Jewish people that Jesus is the king of a different type of kingdom and that those of all nations should become a part of this new kingdom, the church.

Characteristics

Matthew's writing is very concise. His is the only gospel to mention the word "church." Matthew uses ninety percent of Mark, which takes up about fifty percent of Matthew. Twenty-seven percent of Matthew comes from a common source with Luke. Twenty-two percent of his material is unique to Matthew. Matthew quotes from the Old Testament more than sixty times. He uses direct quotes and a formula quotation—"this was done that it might be fulfilled through the prophet saying...." Matthew is keen to demonstrate that Jesus is the fulfillment of OT prophecy.

Jewish Life in the Time of Jesus

In Jesus' day around one-and-a-half to two million Jews lived in Palestine. Around four million others were part of the Diaspora—Jews spread throughout the world. Ninety percent of the Jews of Palestine were the *Am ha-aretz* or the people of the land. These were poor people who scraped together a day-to-day existence. The other ten percent were the political leaders and the landed gentry. The gap between the "haves" and "have-nots" was clearly marked in Jesus' day.

Jewish attitudes toward Rome in the first century:

• The Jews were heavily taxed, and they paid the taxes reluctantly.

• Even though the Jews were hostile to Rome, Rome accepted Judaism as a recognized and legal religion in the Empire. The Romans were not allowed to set up their standard (the eagle) in Jerusalem.

• Less than forty years after Jesus died on the cross, Jerusalem was razed to the ground because of the civil unrest of the Jews.

Matthew also emphasized Jesus as teacher. His gospel contains the longest block of teaching material found in the Gospels: the Sermon on the Mount (Matthew 5-7). The teaching discourses of Jesus comprise three-fifths of Matthew's material.

Several aspects of Matthew are distinctive to his gospel. Matthew uses the term "kingdom of heaven" thirty-three times. Only five times does he speak of the "kingdom of God." Matthew is the only writer to include the following stories:

- The visit of the Magi (Matthew 2:1-16)
- The flight to Egypt and massacre of the infants (Matthew 2:13-18)
- After the Crucifixion, the ground shakes, the tombs open and holy people go into the city (Matthew 27:50-53)
- The bribery of the guards at the tomb (Matthew 28:12-15)
- The miracle of the two blind men (Matthew 20:29-34)
- The healing of the dumb demoniac (Matthew 9:32-33)
- The story of the coin in the fish's mouth (Matthew 17:24-27). Jesus' use of the word "church" (Matthew 16:18, Matthew 18:17).

The Gospel of John

We must put John in a category all his own. His gospel is organized differently and approaches the story of Jesus from a different angle from the Synoptic Gospels.

Authorship

The best sources lead us to the conclusion that John was the last surviving apostle. He was one of the sons of Zebedee, a fisherman of Galilee. His mother was Salome, probably a sister of Mary, Jesus' mother (Matthew 27:56, Mark 15:40, John 19:25). John was a fisherman by trade. He may have belonged to the first disciples of John the Baptist.

John was known as one of the "sons of thunder," also translated, "sons of tumult" (Mark 3:17), and yet he was eventually known to the church as "the apostle of love." The author of John never gives his name, but refers to himself in five places as "the disciple whom Jesus loved." When we note that John, so obviously in Jesus' inner circle in the other gospels (e.g. Mark 9:2; 14:33) is not mentioned by name in this gospel, we have great, even overwhelming, evidence for John's authorship.

John occupied the place of privilege and intimacy at the Last Supper (John 13:23). Jesus committed his own mother to John's care while Jesus was on the cross (John 19:26-27). He was one of the first visitors at the empty tomb. History indicates that he probably died at the end of the first century.

Date and Place of Writing

John probably wrote his gospel during his final years in Ephesus. The gospel has been dated anywhere from AD 40 to 140. The liberals once dated it into the 200s until the John Rylands fragment was found. This small section from John's gospel (18:31-33) was dated somewhere between AD 115 and 135 and is the oldest piece of NT material that we have. Therefore, the gospel had to be written well before these dates since the find was made in Egypt. Most conservative scholars date it late in the first century, around AD 90.

Audience

John addressed a wide range of Gentile Christian readers who were scattered across the Mediterranean world.

Purpose

> Many other signs therefore did Jesus in the presence of the disciples, which are not written in this book: but these are written that you may believe that Jesus is the Christ, the Son of God; and that by believing you may have life in his name. (John 20:30-31, author's translation)

John was apologetic in his writing. He wrote to create faith in Jesus. Given some of the issues the early church had to contend with late in the first century, it would seem that John's gospel was written to defend Jesus against the teachers of Docetism and Gnosticism. The Gnostics believed that the world was evil and wicked by nature. In their minds, God's son could not become flesh without being contaminated by the evil of the material world. Therefore, Jesus only *seemed* to become flesh. "Docetism" comes from the Greek, meaning "to seem". But John states clearly that the Word became flesh and dwelt among us (John 1:14). John portrays Jesus as fully human and fully divine.

John demonstrates the divine nature of Jesus in the "I am" statements that he scatters across his gospel. These statements tie in with the identity of God given to Moses before the burning bush in Exodus: "I AM" (Exodus 3:1-14). Jesus uses this phrase to identify himself in several passages:

- I am the bread of life.   John 6:35
- I am the light of the world.   John 8:12, 9:5
- I am the door (of the sheepfold).   John 10:7 (KJV)
- I am the good shepherd.   John 10:11, 14
- I am the resurrection and the life.   John 11:25
- I am the way and the truth and the life.   John 14:6
- I am the true vine.   John 15:1

Characteristics

Several characteristics separate John from the synoptic Gospels.

- John is arranged by feasts in which Jesus travels from Galilee to Jerusalem (north to south).
- Belief and faith are used ninety-eight times in John. Belief is equivalent to obedience.
- John is written in a more narrative style than the synoptic Gospels.
- John's gospel is more theological than the synoptics.
- The two most important words for understanding John are (1) "believe" which is used ninety-eight times in John (only thirty-four in the synoptics); and (2) "life" which is used thirty-six times in John (only sixteen in the synoptics).
- Merrill Tenney states, "John contains no parables and only seven miracles, five of which are not recorded elsewhere."[6]

The Acts of the Apostles

Acts is not a gospel, but it clearly is a continuation of the Jesus story written as a companion volume to one of the gospels. It begins with Jesus' postresurrection appearances and then shows how the early church was begun and then continued the mission of Jesus, under the power of the Holy Spirit.

Authorship

The author does not identify himself by name, but the evidence points to Luke. The "we" sections of Acts (16:10-17, 20:5-15, 21:1-18, 27:1-28:16) place the author as one of Paul's traveling companions. When we compare the names mentioned in Acts with the names we have in Paul's letters, the name that is obviously missing is Luke.

Date and Place

Written shortly after the gospel of Luke, it is placed around AD 68-69. Like the gospel, Acts was perhaps written from Rome.

Audience

Luke wrote to Gentile Christians in the Roman empire.

Purpose

Some scholars say that Acts was prepared as a legal brief for Paul's trial in Rome. Perhaps *Theophilus* was a Christian lawyer, and Luke was helping him build his case for Paul. Whether this idea is true or not, Luke was defending the Christian faith in Acts. Luke attempts to show that Christianity is politically innocent and morally blameless.

In Corinth, Gallio found the Christians innocent from any crimes (Acts 18:14). In Ephesus, the recorder dispersed the mob and defended the Christians (Acts 19:37). Later, Claudius Lysias told Felix that Paul had done nothing to deserve imprisonment (Acts 23:29). Also, Festus told Agrippa that Paul had done nothing to deserve death (Acts 25:25). Agrippa, Bernice and Festus agreed that Paul could have been released except that he appealed to Caesar (Acts 26:32). All of these voices combine to say that Paul and the early disciples were innocent. They had not broken Roman law.

C. H. Dodd, author of *The Apostolic Preaching and Its Developments,* mentions several other reasons why Acts was circulated.

1. To show that Christianity was not politically dangerous

2. To show the proper relationship between Judaism and Christianity

3. To show that Christianity is for everyone

4. To document the Christian movement from the birth of Jesus to the evangelization of Rome[7]

Characteristics

Acts of the Apostles could also be titled, "The Acts of the Holy Spirit." The Spirit plays a major role in Acts. In Acts 1:4-5, the disciples of Christ are waiting in Jerusalem for the Spirit. The Spirit comes upon the apostles in Acts 2, empowering them to preach the message of Jesus. The qualification of an office bearer is that they are to be men of the Spirit (Acts 6:3). The Spirit directs Philip to the Ethiopian eunuch (Acts 8:27-29). The Spirit tells the church at Antioch to select Barnabas and Paul for mission work (Acts 13:2). Then the Spirit tells the church to open its doors to the Gentiles (Acts 15:19-29). God's Spirit also guides the footsteps of Paul to Europe (Acts 16:6-7).

How important is the book of Acts for our understanding of first century Christianity? Without Acts we would have no information about the earliest days of the church and little information about how the message of Jesus was spread by disciples across the Roman world. Acts describes for us those vital years from AD 30 to 60. This makes Acts a book of extreme importance.

Notes

1. Merrill Tenney, *New Testament Survey, Revised.* (Grand Rapids: Wm. B. Eerdmans Publishing Co., 1985), 163.

2. F. F. Bruce, *The Message of the New Testament* (Exeter, England: The Paternoster Press, 1972), 19-20.

3. Tenney, 177.

4. Ibid., 179.

5. Ibid., 150-151.

6. Ibid., 188.

7. C. H. Dodd, *The Apostolic Preaching and Its Developments* (New York: Harper and Brothers, 1937), 48.

12

The Ministry and Letters of Paul

After the Gospels and Acts, the New Testament is composed of twenty-one letters and the book of Revelation, which itself contains letters to several individual churches. Thirteen of the twenty-one letters come from Paul, the former Saul of Tarsus. No OT books are letters, but letters were written in the early church because of the need for leaders to communicate with geographically separated congregations. (See figure 7 for the best estimate of when each of the letters was written.)

Introduction to Paul

The Jerusalem Council (Acts 15) occurred around AD 49 or 50. Paul's previous visit to Jerusalem was fourteen years earlier around AD 35. Paul was converted three years prior to that—around AD 32 or 33. (See Galatians 1:17-18, 2:1.) He was responsible for writing one-fourth of the New Testament.

Paul was born Saul of Tarsus and was a Roman citizen. His conversion was not from one god to another god; no one tried to please God more than Saul did. Saul had a revelation which changed him. He trained as a Pharisee in Jerusalem under Gamaliel, a liberal rabbi. However, Paul did not inherit Gamaliel's looseness toward tradition. While Gamaliel was advising the Jews to wait and see what the Christian sect would do, Paul was actively persecuting the sect. Paul, by his own admission, was a Pharisee of Pharisees. Acts 23:6 shows that Paul's father was also a Pharisee. The conversion of this fiercely devoted Jew into the chief advocate of the gospel of Jesus still stands as one of the greatest evidences for Jesus' reality.

THE NEW TESTAMENT LETTERS		
Paul's Letters		**Other Letters**
AD 48		*James*
AD 49	*Galatians*	
AD 50	*1-2 Thessalonians*	
AD 55	*1-2 Corinthians*	
AD 56	*Romans*	
AD 60	*Ephesians, Colossians, Philemon, Philippians (Prison Epistles)*	
AD 63-67	*1 Timothy, Titus, 2 Timothy (Pastorals)*	*1-2 Peter*
Late 60s		*Hebrews, 1-3 John, Jude*
AD 69-79		*Revelation*

Figure 7

After his conversion, Paul saw himself as a Christian and as a Jew. Even though he was a Jew, Paul's mission was to the Gentiles. Paul defended the Gentiles against the Judaizers, those Jewish Christians who believed that the Gentiles had to first become Jews before they could become Christians. Paul included three autobiographical sections in his letters (Philippians 3:4-11, Galatians 1-2 and 2 Corinthians 11).

Acts describes at least three missionary journeys of Paul. His work was composed of two phases. In phase one, he would establish a church. In phase two, he would consolidate and strengthen the disciples of Christ at those new plantings.

There are several things we can say about Paul from Acts and from his letters: (1) He spoke and wrote with authority; (2) he loved the churches; (3) he was versatile—1 Corinthians 9:22, "all things to all men"; (4) he was a man of great conviction; (5) his language and style were rough; and (5) his method was not that of an armchair theologian—he was involved with people. His story is one of the most remarkable in human history.

Although this represents something of an oversimplification, Paul's thirteen letters are often grouped into four different categories. (See also figure 8.)
- Eschatological (about the last days): 1 and 2 Thessalonians
- Soteriological (about salvation): Galatians, 1 and 2 Corinthians and Romans

- Prison: Philippians, Philemon, Colossians and Ephesians
- Pastoral: 1 Timothy, Titus and 2 Timothy

Galatians: Christian Freedom

Date and Place

Galatians was written around AD 49, about the time of the Jerusalem Council. Some date Galatians around 53-55, from Ephesus.

Audience

The term "Galatia" can refer to two different places. It could mean the name for the old province of Galatia in the north. New Testament scholar J. B. Lightfoot favors this view. A great migration came across the mountains of Europe from Gaul into Galatia in approximately 400 BC. These were the Galli, or the Celts, whose descendants spoke Gaelic, Erse, Welsh, Cornish and Breton. Barclay says, "They were a wild and terrifying people."[1] By 230 BC they had been confined to a strip of country in the northeast called Galatia, whose three principle cities were Pessinus, Tavium and Ancyra.

The term "Galic" has the same root as the word "Galatia." Galatia came to mean an ethnic group, the Celts. In 29 BC the last king of Galatia, Amyntas, turned Galatia into a Roman territory. Rome expanded Galatia into all of the northern part of Asia Minor, adding Lyconia, Isauria, southeast Phrygia and parts of Pisidia, Pontus and Paphlagonia. The name "Galatia" stood for both the ancient kingdom in the north and the Roman province in the north and south. When Paul was writing, the term "Galatian" was used as an ethnic slur. Paul established churches in north Galatia on his third missionary journey. If

FITTING THE PAULINE EPISTLES INTO ACTS	
Acts 18:5	*1 Thessalonians*
Acts 18:6-18	*2 Thessalonians*
Acts 19:8-22	*Galatians, 1 Corinthians*
Acts 20:1b-2a	*2 Corinthians*
Acts 20:3	*Romans*
Acts 28:30	*Philemon, Colossians, Ephesians, Philippians (Prison Epistles)*
After Acts	*1 Timothy, Titus and 2 Timothy (Pastorals)*

Figure 8

he was writing then, the book could be dated late, as late as AD 55 (see Acts 16:6-8, 18:23).

Galatia could refer to the south: the actual cities that were visited by Paul. Another scholar, William Ramsey, favors this view. Paul is writing to the province of Galatia. He went to southern Asia on the first mission journey in Acts 13-14 and then he wrote the book in AD 49, around the time of this campaign. Ramsey believes that the events in Acts 15 occurred after Galatians 2. So Galatians must have been written early, before the Jerusalem Council.

When Paul arrived in Galatia, he was a sick man (Galatians 4:13). He was suffering from his *skolops*, his thorn in the flesh (2 Corinthians 12:7). The word more accurately means "stake" instead of "thorn." What was it? Scholars have made many suggestions, including eye trouble, epilepsy and chronic malaria. We do not know the exact nature of his ailment, but we do know that Paul saw it as a gift from God to keep him humble.

Purpose

Some time after Paul left Galatia, Paul's doctrine and apostleship were attacked. In this letter he reacts to the accusations. Galatians and 2 Corinthians are the most polemical books of Paul. In both he offers a strong defense of his apostleship. Paul defends his authority in Galatians. Galatians begins with these words: *Paulos apostolos*. His second word is "apostle." Paul wanted his audience to know that he was not in anyone's pocket—he depended only on Jesus. He answered his critics by showing them the scars he had received from persecution (6:17). Paul was the genuine article; he was not a fake.

Paul saw the problem arising in the early church: the Judaizers. They wanted to enforce Jewish laws on Gentile Christians and put the emphasis in the spiritual life on human effort (Galatians 3:1-3). In other words, for Gentiles to become Christians, they also had to become Jews and devote themselves to the law. If Paul had lost the battle to the Judaizers, then Christianity would have become just a subsect of Judaism—and the cross would be no more significant than circumcision would.

Galatians is the "Declaration of Independence" of Christianity—it offers freedom. One Biblical writer has noted, "Galatians is not a sermon, it is not a treatise; it is a sword-cut, delivered in the hour of extreme peril by a combatant assailed by dangerous foes."[2] Paul wants to protect the Gentile churches from the Judaizers. Galatians is his attempt to do that.

Characteristics

Who were the opponents of Paul in this letter? They were either Jews or Jewish Christians. These people made Jewish customs a test of fellowship. Paul deals with the Judaizers by:

- Showing that obeying the law does not make one righteous—Paul had obeyed and it did not make him righteous. For Paul, the law was no longer a means to salvation.
- Showing that when people are in Christ, the distinction between Jew and Greek is lost. The gospel conquers ethnic and racial barriers.
- Teaching that Christians should not observe empty religious rituals. The disciple of Jesus is too engaged in well-doing and fostering brotherhood to be shackled by ritual.
- Refining the true Israel. Jews said circumcision was a sign of their covenant with God. Paul said that faith distinguishes Israel. He showed that the law was given after Abraham (Galatians 3:19— added for transgression). Abraham lived four hundred years before Moses. Abraham was faithful before the law.
- Using the allegory of Sarah and Hagar to demonstrate that Judaism is the child of slavery, but freedom comes in Christ (4:24ff).
- Giving stern exhortations (4:1ff). Paul does not want his labor to have been in vain.

1 and 2 Thessalonians: The Present Is Important

Date and Place

Paul wrote 1 Thessalonians between AD 50-51. This can be dated with certainty because of the Delphi inscription, which shows that Gallio came to Corinth as proconsul in AD 51 or 52 (Acts 18:12-17). When Paul was taken before Gallio, he was writing to Thessalonica (Acts 18:12-18). There were probably three to six months between the penning of the first and second letters to the Thessalonians.

Audience

Paul wrote to a church made up predominately of Gentile Christians with pagan backgrounds. Thessalonica was one of the great cities of the ancient world. The city was founded by the king of Macedon in 315 BC and named for his wife. Thessalonica then quickly surpassed her neighbors to become the principal city in Macedonia. Thessalonica was a port city located on the Gulf of Solanika on one of the greatest Roman roads—the Egnatian way, which was the main highway from the East to Rome. The main street of Thessalonica was part of this road. It reached east to Byzantium and west to Rome. It was an industrial, maritime and commercial city. It was also the capital of the Macedonian province, a city of seventy thousand inhabitants, of whom twenty thousand were Jews.

The first place where the Apostle Paul drew a significant response from influential people to his preaching was in Thessalonica. People of social influence were drawn to his message. Just like in the first century, prominent people are drawn to the word of God today. With this type of response, it is understandable that certain people began an effort to oppose Paul and we should not expect that this will be any different today. The opponents of Paul forced the government to step in and escort him from Thessalonica, having been there for only three short weeks. He was concerned about how the church would fare in his absence. His two letters back to Thessalonica, written soon after his forced departure from the city, display the concern that he had for a young church which was undergoing hardship from the same people that had opposed him. Would this church hold up under the pressure? Paul was certain that they would.

How did Paul end up in Thessalonica? After the Council of Jerusalem in AD 49, Paul went on a second missionary journey with Silas. Acts 16 records that Paul went to Philippi, but the Philippians ran Paul out of town because they did not want to hear his message. In Acts 17 Paul went to Thessalonica. He converted many people, especially Gentiles, before the Jews ran him out of that town, after having been there for three weeks. He then went to Berea, where he began to make progress with the Bereans, but the Jews from Thessalonica followed him to Berea and caused trouble for him there. Next, he moved to Athens. While in Athens, he sent Timothy to Thessalonica. After Athens, Paul went to Corinth. Silas and Timothy came to Paul in Corinth and reported to him (Acts 18:5). Paul wrote both his letters to the Thessalonians from Corinth, where he lived for eighteen months.

Purpose

In 1 Thessalonians 3:10, Paul writes, "Night and day we pray most earnestly that we may see you again and supply what is lacking in your faith." Because Paul had to leave Thessalonica so abruptly, he was unable to teach the church very much about discipleship. He was concerned about their response to the persecution that had forced him to leave. He also was concerned with the report Timothy gave him in Corinth, and he wanted to correct some of the things he heard from him. He was writing to fill in the gaps of their faith.

Characteristics

Paul was anxious about his new work in Thessalonica for several reasons. First of all, could a community of Christians grow up in three weeks? William Barclay states, It has always been true that Christianity is caught not taught, and the saving and changing power of the Gospel made it spread like a contagion wherever it went.[3]
Paul was able to build a dynamic ministry in twenty-one short days, but the disciples needed to be strengthened—thus the two letters to the Thessalonians.

Second, a charge against Paul's character was made in Thessalonica (1 Thessalonians 2:1-12). They were saying that he was deceitful, that he pleased men with flattery, and that he was greedy, domineering and dictatorial. Paul responds to these charges in 1 Thessalonians 2:9-12 and 2 Thessalonians 3:7-10.

Third, Paul also needed to direct the Thessalonians in their understanding of the Second Coming of Jesus. Their focus on the Second Coming had led many of them to leave their work and disrupt their ordinary life activities. They did nothing but stand about watching the sky and talking about Jesus' coming. They were the laughingstock of their community and a burden to the church (1 Thessalonians 4:11-12; 2 Thessalonians 3:6-13). Paul corrects their understanding, telling them to get back to work because no one knew exactly when Jesus would come.

1 Corinthians: Fixing Problems
Date and Place

Paul wrote 1 Corinthians between AD 53-55 from Ephesus (1 Corinthians 16:8, 19).

Audience

In 146 BC, the Romans destroyed Corinth. Later, Julius Caesar rebuilt it and Augustus made it the capital of the province of Achaia. In Paul's day it was as important as Athens. The Acropolis sat on top of a sacred area in the center of Acrocorinth. The Temple of Aphrodite, the Greek goddess of love, was located in this area of Corinth. The temple was known throughout the region as a bastion of immorality and almost single-handedly marked Corinth as the most pagan city in the Mediterranean world. This temple had more than a thousand sacred prostitutes. To have intercourse with one of these women was considered an act of worship. In Paul's day, Corinthians were thought to be libertines, promiscuous and without morals. Corinth was considered a very pagan place. For Paul, a pagan population represented an open field. Perhaps this is why he stayed in this city for eighteen months (one of his longest periods of residence on his missionary tours).

Corinth was a city of two hundred thousand citizens and five hundred thousand slaves, a total of seven hundred thousand inhabitants. It was one of the greatest commercial and industrial cities of the ancient world. It was well known for the production of ceramics. Greece was almost cut in two by the Corinthian and Saronic Gulfs. Between them was an isthmus no more than five miles wide, and Corinth stood on that isthmus. It was the bridge of Greece. Every item of north-south trade passed through it. On east-west travel, ships were hauled over Corinth from one sea to the other on rollers.

The church in Corinth was founded by Paul on his second missionary journey in AD 49-51 (probably 50). Acts 18 tells about Paul's ministry in Corinth. Paul stayed with Aquila and Priscilla. He first preached to the Jews and then to the Gentiles. He later lived with Titus Justus in his house by the synagogue. He met the proconsul Gallio there. In Acts 20:31 we have reference that while Paul was on his third journey in the city of Ephesus, he began the Corinthian correspondence.

Purpose

While in Ephesus, Paul discovered that the Corinthian church had developed many problems. He wrote them one letter, which had no effect upon them. He then wrote them a second letter (our letter of 1 Corinthians) to see if he could encourage change in the church.

Characteristics

Paul's correspondence to the church in Corinth may have consisted of four letters, not two. The first letter has not survived. Paul mentions it as his "previous letter" in 1 Corinthians 5:9. After writing this first letter, Paul received a report about the church from Chloe (1 Corinthians 1:11). He also received a letter from the church in Corinth (1 Corinthians 7:1). Paul then sat down and wrote a second letter to the church in Corinth. This is our book of 1 Corinthians.

Paul made a journey to Corinth from Ephesus on his third missionary journey. Upon arrival back in Ephesus, Paul writes a third letter to Corinth. This is known as his stern or sorrowful letter. It was sent by Titus (2 Corinthians 7:6-16) to the church in Corinth. Many scholars believe that this letter is contained in 2 Corinthians 10-13.

Paul wrote a fourth letter to the church from Macedonia. Titus gave Paul a good report on his return from Corinth after delivering the third letter (the stern letter) to them. Paul was delighted to hear of the changes in the church in Corinth so he penned a fourth letter to the church, congratulating the disciples on their changes. Many believe that this fourth letter is contained in 2 Corinthians 1-9. After this encouraging fourth letter, Paul makes a third trip to Corinth and pens the book of Romans while staying there. Thus we have the saga of the four letters to Corinth—one which was lost and three which may have ended up as two letters in our canon. We must be quick to add, however, that no manuscript evidence has been found to support the idea that our present letter of 2 Corinthians is a combination of two separate documents.

Paul addressed many problems in 1 Corinthians.
- A partisan spirit (1 Corinthians 1:10-11, 3:3-15): Apollos—intellectualism; Peter—legalism; Paul—libertinism
- Intellectual pride (1:17, 1:20-25, 2:1-5, 2:10-16, 3:18-23)
- Immorality (1 Corinthians 5)—a man was living with his stepmother
- Legal disputes (6:1-8)
- Antinomianism (6:9-20): the belief that the body is bad, the soul is good—so, do whatever you want with your body
- Problems in marriage and sexual relations (1 Corinthians 7)
- Meat offered to idols (1 Corinthians 8-10)
- Role of women in the church (11:1-16, 14:34-36)
- Abusing the Lord's Supper (11:17-34)
- Problems with spiritual gifts (1 Corinthians 12-14)
- Problem of the resurrection of the body (1 Corinthians 15)

The Corinthian church faced a myriad of problems, but many of them were rooted in a tendency that this Greek church had of moving away from the centrality of the cross. Paul knew that most of their issues would be resolved by showing others the love we see at the cross (1 Corinthians 13), and so he wrote,

> For I resolved to know nothing while I was with you except
> Jesus Christ and him crucified. (1 Corinthians 2:2)

2 Corinthians: Joy and Pain
Date and Place
2 Corinthians was written in AD 56 from the province of Macedonia (2 Corinthians 2:12-13, 2 Corinthians 7:5, 2 Corinthians 8:1, 2 Corinthians 9:2-4). Paul met Titus in Macedonia and learned more about the church in Corinth. He directed another correspondence to them in response to the news from Titus. He especially answers attacks upon his character in this letter.

Audience
The disciples of Christ in Corinth were again Paul's audience.

Purpose
Paul wrote to encourage the disciples because of the changes they had made (2 Corinthians 1-9). In the last three chapters (10-13), Paul rebukes them for their lack of change, and he answers criticisms of his apostleship. As already noted, because these sections are so different, many scholars believe that two separate letters of Paul have been placed into one book.

Characteristics
Paul defends his apostleship in 2 Corinthians. What were the some of the criticisms leveled against Paul?
- He was unstable (2 Corinthians 1:15ff).
- His letters were unclear (2 Corinthians 1:13ff).
- He didn't have a letter of recommendation (2 Corinthians 3:1).
- His gospel was not clear (2 Corinthians 4:3).
- His behavior was offensive (2 Corinthians 10:2).
- He harmed the community and enriched himself (2 Corinthians 7:2).
- He did not belong to Christ (2 Corinthians 10:7).
- He was a pitiful speaker (2 Corinthians 11:6).
- He came to Corinth without an appropriate order or commission (2 Corinthians 10:13ff).
- He was inferior to the "superior" apostles (2 Corinthians 12:11, 11:5).
- He was actually no apostle at all (2 Corinthians 12:12).
- The most stinging criticism was that Christ did not speak through him (2 Corinthians 13:3).

While Paul does defend himself against these charges, he also is more vulnerable and open in this letter than in any other (2 Corinthians 1:8-11, 2:4, 2:12-13, 4:7-9, 6:11-12). Perhaps nothing Paul wrote gives us such a clear idea of his conviction about how God works powerfully in our weaknesses (12:7-10). Chapters 8 and 9 give us the unique and inspiring principles that lead to Christian generosity.

Romans: The Constitution of Christianity
Date and Place
Romans was written from Corinth on Paul's third visit there (Acts 20:2-3), most likely in AD 56. In Romans 15:23-26, Paul said that he was ready to go to Jerusalem in order to deliver the great collection for the poor (1 Corinthians 16:1-2, 2 Corinthians 8 and 9).

Audience
Paul did not plant the church in Rome (Romans 1:8-13). There have been several suggestions about who might have played that role.

- Peter—This is not likely. Paul does not mention Peter in the book of Romans, and there is no evidence of him coming to Rome until the 60s.
- Jewish converts who were at Pentecost (Acts 2:10). They went back home to Rome with the message of Christ and began the church through their preaching.
- Christians from several backgrounds who ended up in the cosmopolitan city of Rome. Disciples of Jesus from all over the Empire would have traveled to Rome for various reasons. While there, they met together and began the church in Rome.

Romans 1:13 and 15:23 imply that the church in Rome existed many years before Paul wrote the letter. Suetonius, a historian, tells of Jewish riots in AD 49. He connects these with a man named *Chrestus*, probably meaning Christ. Claudius, the Roman emperor, made the Jews leave Rome in AD 49. Aquila and Priscilla were forced out at this point (Acts 18:2). One can make arguments that the congregation was mainly Jewish (Romans 2:17-3:8, 3:21-31, 4:1, 6:1-7:6, chapters 9-11, 14:1-15:3) or mainly Gentile (Romans 1:5- 6, 13; 6:19; 10:1).

Rome was considered the greatest city of the first-century world, traditionally established in 753 BC. Men of influence from around the world were attracted to Rome because of its military might and its economic strength. Whereas Greece was known for its advancement in the arts and sciences, Rome was noted for its ability to borrow the best aspects of Greek and other cultures. Rome was not a great innovator. However, the Greeks had brought civilization to a point at which Rome could build upon its accomplishments.

In the first century, Rome was a bustling, growing city. It was home to at least a million working class people, with an aristocracy that benefited from investments on three separate continents. Rome became the central hub for trade throughout all of Asia, Africa and Europe. The Roman Empire began and ended with the great city of Rome. It was the diplomatic capital of the Empire, serving as home to diplomats from all of the Roman states. Simply put, first-century Rome was the center of civilization.

The apostle Paul is first mentioned in connection with Rome in Acts 18:2. Here he met two Jews, Aquila and Priscilla, who had left Rome when the Emperor Claudius issued an edit that expelled all the Jews from Rome. Paul's heart burned for the city. He had preached in many great cities, but he longed to preach in the city that was the center of the Roman world.

Paul's desire to visit Rome is mentioned in Acts 19:21. By reading Romans, we can see that Paul knew many of the disciples at Rome. Many of the names that he mentions are Jewish names. No doubt Paul had met many of them in Jerusalem before he became a disciple. Other names are not Jewish. It appears that the church in Rome contained both Jewish and Gentile Christians. It seems that Paul wrote Romans as a letter of introduction in preparation for his trip to Rome. He knew that most of the church had undoubtedly heard of him, but he wanted them to know firsthand the heart if his message.

Purpose

Paul may have written to Rome in an attempt to head off the Jewish/Gentile controversy there. He had not been to Rome, and he wished the church there to know him and his theology. Paul gives a comprehensive statement of his theology in the book of Romans. This becomes his letter of introduction to the church in Rome. He wrote them to let them know that he was coming and to request help to get to Spain (Romans 1:10-15, 15:14-33).

Characteristics

Romans has been called the Magna Carta of Christianity. Paul expresses the essence of Christianity by echoing a phrase borrowed from the Old Testament, "The righteous shall live by faith." This is the gospel according to Paul. Living by faith gives us freedom: freedom from sin, freedom from the law and freedom from death. However, this freedom does not give us a license to sin. On the contrary, it calls us to a higher ethic and a higher responsibility to the church, the world and the state. Because Jesus died on the cross, we have the freedom to live a righteous life in Christ. In Romans, Paul proclaims this freedom.

The Prison Letters

Four of Paul's letters were all written from prison and probably in this order:
1.   Philemon 1, 9-10, 13, 23
2.   Colossians 4:3, 10, 18
3.   Ephesians 3:1, 4:1, 6:20
4.   Philippians 1:7, 1:13-14

Which imprisonment was Paul enduring when he wrote these letters? Some scholars believe that Paul wrote them during his two-year imprisonment in Caesarea during AD 56-58. But this is not acceptable because Paul mentions in Philemon 22 that he was about to be released. Paul had no hope of being released until he got to Rome.

Paul was in prison in Rome between AD 60-62. He was released after this and continued his mission work until he was arrested and executed under Nero. These prison epistles fit best within the context of Paul's imprisonment in Rome.

Philemon: Treat Him As a Brother
Date and Place
Paul wrote from prison, in Rome (AD 60).

Audience
Philemon, the owner of Onesimus, was the recipient of this letter.

Purpose
A man named Onesimus was a slave who ran away from Philemon. Onesimus finds Paul in Rome. Verse 10 of Philemon tells us that Paul

converted Onesimus. He sends Onesimus back to Philemon. Paul writes this letter to tell Philemon how to treat Onesimus now that he is a brother.

Philemon demonstrates the importance of relationships within the church. Although Paul as an apostle could have ordered Philemon to receive Onesimus back without penalty, he appeals to Philemon as a brother in the faith. He reminds Philemon of his own debt toward Paul. Rather than ordering Philemon to do what is right, Paul influences Philemon to do the right thing.

Onesimus was from Colossae (Colossians 4:9). He could have been a thief as well as a runaway slave because Paul notes,

> If he has wronged you at all, or owes you anything, charge that to my account. I, Paul, write this with my own hand, I will repay it—to say nothing of your owing me even your own self. (Philemon 18-19 RSV).

During the New Testament time, there were more than sixty million slaves in the Roman Empire. A slave was not considered a person. The master could do anything he wanted to his slave—scourge, imprison, mutilate or kill. The writer Augustus relates one story. He writes concerning a man who lost his fortune. After losing his fortune, this man still possessed 4,160 slaves. Another story speaks about a day in Petronius's house when thirty boys and forty girls were born to slaves. A slave was the property of the master. If a master were murdered, all his slaves were to be executed. In the case of Pedianus Secundus, this totaled more than four hundred men. When runaway slaves were caught, they were either crucified or branded with the letter "F" on their foreheads for *fugitivus,* which means "fugitive."

Colossians: The Supremacy of Christ
Date and Place
Paul wrote this letter from prison, in Rome (AD 60).

Audience
Colossae was one hundred miles east of Ephesus. It was in the Lycus valley and was overshadowed by the city of Laodicea. Colossians 1:4 and 2:1 demonstrate that Paul never visited Colossae. Epaphras, one of Paul's fellow workers (Colossians 1:7, 4:12-13), might have founded the church

there. Colossae was part of a tri-city area, which included Colossae, Laodicea and Hierapolis.

The mixture of Jewish, Greek and Phrygian elements in the population of the city were probably found also in the church: it would have been fertile ground for the type of speculative heresy which Paul's letter was designed to counter.

The neighborhood was devastated by an earthquake, dated by Tacitus (*Ann.* 14.27) to AD 60. There is no hint of this in Colossians, which we must suppose was written before news of the disaster had reached Rome.

Purpose

The key theme in Colossians is that Christ is preeminent (supreme). Paul was in prison in Rome from AD 60-62. In Philemon 23, Epaphras is noted as a fellow prisoner of Paul. Epaphras must have shared with Paul that some in Colossae were teaching that something else is needed in addition to Christ. Archipus (Colossians 4:17) was the minister in Colossae when Epaphras went to Rome. For some reason, Epaphras was not ready to return to Colossae, so Tychicus and Onesimus took the letter with them. The letter battles the false teaching that was being spread to the church in Colossae.

Characteristics

What was the heresy at Colossae? It cannot be identified for certain, but some characteristics of it are given as follows:

- Faulty Christology (Colossians 2:8)
- Philosophic undertones (Colossians 2:8)
- Jewish rituals (Colossians 2:16-17)
- Angel worship—Christ may have been seen as only a great angel (Colossians 2:18)
- Astrology
- Elements of worldliness
- Feeling of exclusivity
- Special knowledge = Gnosticism
- Ascetic tendencies (Colossians 2:22-23)

Many of the characteristics fit with a false teaching called Gnosticism. In the mid-1940s, the Nag Hammadi Library containing Gnostic texts was found, helping scholars determine that full-blown Gnosticism did not come until the second century. What we find in the background of Colossians and other NT books could be a form of incipient Gnosticism. How did Paul address this heresy? He draws attention away from the heresy and to the person of Christ.

- Christ is the center of creation.
- Christ possesses all wisdom and knowledge.
- Christ is superior to angelic beings.
- Paul indicates that in the death and resurrection of Jesus, a final victory has been gained over all opposing forces.

Ephesians: Glory in the Church
Date and Place

From prison, in Rome (AD 60), Paul wrote to the church in Ephesus.

Audience

Ephesus was one of the greatest cities of the ancient world. The Apostle Paul recognized its importance, and he was determined to build a great church there. It was (1) a maritime city, (2) a gateway to the interior of Asia Minor, and (3) the home of the Temple of Diana (Artemis)—one of the seven wonders of the ancient world.

Again we see Paul choosing one of the great cities of the ancient world from which to launch a ministry. Ephesus was known for many things, including its fine harbor. It provided a great port that encouraged trade within the city, and made Ephesus a commercial center. Cutting through the center of Ephesus was a columned road that went for a distance of eleven miles. This road had been used for centuries as a highway that linked Ephesus with Rome and Asia. This made Ephesus a literal crossroads and a perfect city for Paul's ministry. He decided to stay there for three years building a strong pillar church. As far as we know, he stayed there longer than any other place on his missionary tours.

Today Ephesus boasts of many great archaeological sites. Much of the ancient city has been uncovered. Archaeologists have discovered houses, gymnasiums, wells, fountains, aqueducts, streets, baths and an impressive library. Many of these finds date to the first century. They would have been the same stones that Paul and the early disciples touched.

The most impressive discovery in Ephesus is a twenty-five thousand seat theater. This theater seated as many people as Madison Square Garden in

New York City does today. It was the site of many theatrical performances in Ephesus, and was also the arena for the gladiatorial games held there. As a public building, it was used for city meetings and public gatherings. We have to wonder if the first century disciples ever met in that theater?

Another great discovery in Ephesus was uncovered by the late archaeologist J. T. Wood in 1870. It has been identified as the temple of Artemis, which is listed as one of the seven wonders of the ancient world. Like Corinth, Ephesus was noted as a center of pagan worship. (It seems that Paul loved to preach in pagan cities). This temple was the largest Greek temple in the ancient world, housing an idol of the goddess Artemis. Some scholars have speculated that the idol might have been an actual meteorite. (Those of us who watch the *X-Files* could make much of this!) One thing is certain, the Temple of Artemis and the theater at Ephesus were two of the most impressive buildings in the ancient world. Ephesus was a city of great standing in the Roman Empire.

The Ephesians took great pride in having the temple of Artemis in their city—after all, it was one of the seven wonders of the world. The worship of Artemis was displayed at all the official activities of the city. The citizens of Ephesus were quick to defend the cult of Artemis against anyone who opposed it. The temple of Artemis contributed in a positive way to the economy of Ephesus. People from all over the region came to Ephesus to worship Artemis and to visit her spectacular temple. While there, they bought sacred trinkets to take back home with them. Because Christianity was such an exclusive religion, it was destined to clash with the cult of Artemis. This clash is recorded in Acts 19, and the central issue in the conflict is not truth or morality, but money. Christianity had grown so much in Ephesus that it hurt the trade of cult objects in the city. How much would the church have to grow in America for us to be able to make economic changes within the country?

The apostle Paul played a key role in taking Christianity to Ephesus. He began by preaching in the synagogues around the city, which was his course of operations in many of the cities where he began a ministry. Paul soon branched out to the lecture hall of Tyrannus. Paul was continuing with his mission to reach out to the Jews first and then to the Greeks.

Ephesus became a pillar church for Paul's ministry to the adjacent cities located in Asia Minor. During his three-year stay in Ephesus, he wrote back to the church in Corinth because he wanted to stay in contact with the churches that he had visited on previous mission trips. This continued his policy of strengthening what had already been planted. Many young ministers must have come through the city to seek Paul's advice during his long stay there.

During his journey to deliver a contribution to the poor disciples of Jerusalem, Paul met with the elders of the church in Ephesus and with tears, bid them good-bye. Paul loved the church in Ephesus. His letter to the church in Ephesus speaks of the glory of the church. Scholars debate as to whether Ephesians was actually written to the church in Ephesus or several churches within that region. Considering the theme of the book—glory in the church—Paul must have been reflecting on his feeling about the church in Ephesus as he penned the book. He certainly considered the church there to be a glorious church.

Purpose

Ephesians glorifies the church more than any other book in the New Testament. Paul writes about the eternal nature of the church. He mentions that the church is the fulfillment of OT prophecy. The church is the continuation of the kingdom concept that was established in the Old Testament. But the kingdom is now a spiritual kingdom that battles against principalities and powers in the heavenly realms. This same kingdom is also described as the body of Christ. Each member is a part of his body. Through this type of language, Paul glorifies the church and allows her members to see how important the church is in God's eternal plan to redeem the world.

Philippians: Joy in All Circumstances

Date and Place

Paul wrote to the Philippians from prison, in Rome (AD 60).

Audience

Phillip of Macedon, father of Alexander the Great, founded Philippi in 350 BC. It was situated on the Egnatian Way—the major Roman highway between Asia and Europe that connected Dyrrachium to Constantinople. (As we have seen earlier, Thessalonica was also located on this road.) The battle between Brutus and Cassius, the last defenders of the Roman Republic, and Mark Antony and Octavian, who became the first emperor, occurred here. Octavian gave the city of Philippi its name and also gave it the full rights of the Roman Empire. This meant that the people living in Philippi enjoyed all the privileges of those who lived in the imperial city of Rome. The Philippians took great pride in their status as true Roman citizens.

It was at Philippi that the ancient Roman Republic died and the new Roman Empire began. Philippi was one of the most fertile plains in the world. It was known for gold and silver mining and was the gateway between Europe and Asia. The city was filled with Roman ex-military people. Augustus made Philippi a Roman colony in 42 BC.

The church in Philippi was the first congregation that Paul planted in Europe. In Acts 16:9, Paul envisions a man from Macedonia who implores him to come to Macedonia and preach. His appeal to Paul, "Come over to Macedonia and help us," must have rung in Paul's ears. He interpreted this as a sign from God. He sailed for Macedonia and arrived in Philippi, which became the hub city for Paul's mission work in that part of the Roman world. In Acts 16 there are four key events in the Philippian church: (1) The conversion of Lydia; (2) the healing of a soothsaying girl; (3) the imprisonment of Paul and Silas; and (4) the conversion of the Philippian jailer.

Acts 20:1-6 tells of Paul's visit to Philippi twice on his third missionary journey. This congregation sent Paul a gift while he was in Thessalonica (Philippians 4:16) and while he was in Corinth (2 Corinthians 11:9) and also while he was in Rome (Philippians 4:18).

Purpose

Paul seems to feel emotionally closer to the Philippian church than any other. The Philippians heard of Paul's imprisonment and sent a gift to Paul by the hands of Epaphroditus, who then stayed with Paul awhile (Philippians 2:25). During this time, Epaphroditus (Philippians 2:27) became sick and almost died. When he recovered, Paul sent him home (Philippians 2:28-29).

Paul's letter to the church is personal, containing some words of correction, but overflowing with joy and encouragement. In the letter he commends Epaphroditus, shares confidence about how his imprisonment will be resolved, thanks them for their gift, and encourages them toward unity and fellowship. The key to such unity is found in chapter 2 in his statement about Jesus. Possibly from an early hymn, it is a classic call for disciples to imitate Jesus' servant leadership.

The Pastoral Epistles

Denominational Christianity uses the word "pastor" (shepherd) to refer to a minister or evangelist. Since 1 and 2 Timothy and Titus were written to young evangelists, the title "Pastoral" has been applied to them. These letters are a bridge between the first and second century church. The letters do not fit into the chronology of Acts. Paul must have written these letters after he was released from prison in Rome in AD 60-61. Paul himself was in his 60s when he wrote these letters, as he considered himself an old man by this point (Philemon 9). The dating of the Pastorals is as follows:

- 1 Timothy = AD 63
- Titus = AD 65
- 2 Timothy = AD 67

All three books had to be written no later than the end of Nero's reign in AD 68 because Paul died during his reign. Liberal scholars doubt if any of these books are from Paul's hand. They list several reasons why they reject Pauline authorship of the Pastorals.

- The vocabulary is too different. But these were written to individuals, not churches. They were written later in Paul's life. Perhaps he had grown as a writer. Imagine how his thinking could have had developed after four years in prison.
- The hierarchy of the church is too developed. But Paul is writing to church leaders who are ready to appoint other church leaders. Church leadership would have developed over time.
- We cannot fit these letters into the chronology of Acts. But these letters were likely written after Acts.

There is no reason to doubt the Pauline authorship of these books.

Where did Paul go after Acts? Perhaps Ephesus? Maybe Crete? He always wanted to travel to Spain, so perhaps Spain? We do not know where Paul went after Acts. But these three letters were written to two of his young evangelists after he was released from prison in Rome.

1 Timothy: In the Household of God
Date and Place

The first letter to Timothy was written around AD 63, but we do not know the place from which it was written.

Audience

This first letter to Timothy was written to Timothy while he was a minister with the church in Ephesus.

Purpose

Paul had several reasons for writing to Timothy.

- To encourage his associate to be faithful in the ministry
- To give instructions about church organization and worship
- To oppose heresy and insist that sound doctrine be preached
- To certify his approval of Timothy
- To make it clear "how one ought to behave in the household of God, which is the church of the living God" (1 Timothy 3:15 RSV)

Timothy, a Biography

Paul mentions Timothy as a cosender of some of his letters. He variously describes him as "our brother," a fellow-worker and a "beloved and faithful child in the Lord." He was a native of Lystra in Asia Minor, the son of a Jewish woman and a Greek man (Acts 16:1-2). His mother, Eunice, and his grandmother, Lois (2 Timothy 1:5), both became Christians probably on Paul's first missionary journey. Timothy may have become a Christian at the same time. His mother had not had him circumcised, perhaps because of the objection of his father, but Timothy was taught the Scriptures from an early age (2 Timothy 3:15).

On Paul's second journey, he selected Timothy as a traveling companion. Paul had Timothy circumcised to make him more effective as a coworker to the Jews (Acts 16:3). At Athens, Paul sends Timothy to Thessalonica to strengthen the church. He is to establish their faith, to assess how they have fared in the persecution and to give Paul's personal greetings. Timothy then joins Paul in Corinth and reports the good news to Paul of the Thessalonican church. He also brings questions from them. Paul responds with 1 Thessalonians.

We next see Timothy in Ephesus with Paul a few years later. Paul decides to send Timothy back to Corinth with a letter, 1 Corinthians. Titus takes over the work in Corinth from Timothy, but on Paul's next visit to Corinth, Timothy is there waiting for him. Timothy then began the journey to Jerusalem with Paul, but we do not know if he went all the way to Jerusalem or not. Timothy was with Paul, helping him as he was imprisoned in Rome, although Timothy was himself free.

The letters to Timothy portray him as youthful, inexperienced, perhaps intimidated by strong opposition and requiring the encouragement and instruction of his mentor on both personal and church matters. Paul is trying to toughen up Timothy.

- 2 Timothy 1:7   "God did not give us a spirit of timidity"
- 2 Timothy 1:8   "do not be ashamed"
- 2 Timothy 2:1   "be strong"
- 2 Timothy 2:3   "endure hardship"
- 1 Timothy 4:12   "do not let anyone look down on you because you are young"

The first letter implies that Timothy was in Ephesus (1 Timothy 1:3). The second letter states that Paul was arrested for a second time and was back in prison in Rome. He asks Timothy and Mark to join him before winter and to bring his cloak. Timothy might have been arrested on this visit as the Hebrew letter speaks of his release from prison.

> I want you to know that our brother Timothy has been released. If he arrives soon, I will come with him to see you. (Hebrews 13:23)

Timothy must have witnessed Paul's death in Rome. According to later tradition, Timothy would go on to continue leading the ministry in Ephesus.

Titus: Devoted to What Is Good

Date and Place

Titus was written in AD 65, but we do not know the place from which the letter originated.

Audience

The letter was written to a young associate of Paul, Titus, while he was a minister in Corinth.

Purpose

Paul's purpose in writing to Titus was to help train Titus in the ministry and to give directions for building strong churches. He is particularly concerned about showing how a true acceptance of the grace of God leads to doing what is good.

Titus, a Biography

Titus was a Gentile Christian (Galatians 2:3) and one of Paul's traveling companions. He worked closely with Paul in the Corinthian church and assisted Paul in the collection for the poor in Jerusalem. Paul chose Titus to accompany him to Jerusalem as he discussed the Jew/Gentile controversy. Titus was Paul's visual aid to the Jewish Christians of his work among the Gentiles, demonstrating his high regard for Titus. Paul did not compel Titus to be circumcised. This served as a test case for the Gentile Christians. If Paul could get Titus to be accepted by the Jerusalem community, then it would help his cause in this controversy. The *Anchor Bible Dictionary* notes, "Titus left Jerusalem as an uncircumcised Gentile, and as such, served as a powerful witness that a Gentile could participate in God's salvation without accepting this prescription of the Torah."[4]

Titus was Paul's strong right arm in the Corinthian church. When news came to Paul that certain men had turned against him in Corinth, Paul sent Titus to deal with the situation. How valuable it is to have someone like this as your assistant. Titus reminded the church of their obedience to the founding apostle (2 Corinthians 7:15).

Paul planned to meet Titus on his return trip in Troas. For some reason, Titus never showed. This disturbed Paul:

> Now when I went to Troas to preach the gospel of Christ and found that the Lord had opened a door for me, I still had no peace of mind, because I did not find my brother Titus there. So I said good-by to them and went on to Macedonia. (2 Corinthians 2:12-13)

Paul continued to be bothered by Titus' absence (2 Corinthians 7:5). They were finally reunited in Macedonia. Paul was comforted by seeing Titus and by hearing that Titus was successful in Corinth.

Paul then sent Titus back to Corinth to assist in the collection for the poor of Jerusalem (2 Corinthians 8:6). Paul also sent two companions with Titus to help (2 Corinthians 8:19-23), showing the importance of this collection in Paul's mind.

Titus is also mentioned as going to Crete to correct a deteriorating situation in the church and to appoint elders.

2 Timothy: Be Strong in the Grace

Date and Place

Paul wrote 2 Timothy in AD 67 from prison in Rome.

Audience

Timothy, who was the minister in Ephesus, was the recipient of Paul's letter.

Purpose

Paul was asking Timothy to meet him in Rome (2 Timothy 4:9, 11, 13, 21), but he uses the letter to give his son in the faith many important reminders of what it takes to stay faithful to the mission. The letter ends with Paul's stirring statement about having finished the race and kept the faith. In his last-ever letter Paul leaves no doubt that the only thing that allows any of us to stand is the grace of God (1:9, 2:1).

Notes

1. William Barclay, *A Beginner's Guide to the New Testament* (Edinburgh: Saint Andrew Press, 1976), 42.

2. Attributed to Gloel in Barclay, 43.

3. Barclay, 62.

4. John Gilman, "Titus" in *The Anchor Bible Dictionary Vol. 6.*, edited by David Noel Freedman (New York: Doubleday, 1992), 581.

13

Hebrews, the General Letters and Revelation

In this chapter we will group together all the New Testament material that we have not yet covered. This will include the letter to the Hebrews, the seven letters often referred to as the "General Letters," and finally, the well-known but misunderstood book of Revelation.

Hebrews: Don't Turn Back

Authorship

The authorship of Hebrews is less certain and more disputed than any other book in the New Testament. The early church father, Origen (c. 254), said of the author of Hebrews, "Who wrote the letter to the Hebrews? God only knows."

What do we know about the author?

- The author was a person with a Jewish background, having an extensive understanding of the Old Testament and the Jewish sacrificial system.
- The author had a thorough knowledge of the Greek language.
- It appears from Hebrews 2:3 that the author must have been one generation removed from Jesus, "This salvation, which was first announced by the Lord, was confirmed to us by those who heard him." This would disqualify all of the apostles, including Paul.
- The author had a personal relationship with Timothy (13:23).

The following are conjectures as to the person who might have written Hebrews.

- Apollos—a Jew of Alexandria with a thorough knowledge of the Scriptures (This was Martin Luther's opinion.)
- Barnabas—from Cyprus, but also a Levite (This was the opinion of Tertullian, an early church leader.)
- Priscilla, the wife of Aquila (This theory was suggested by Harnack, a NT scholar, but without much basis.)
- Luke (Clement of Alexandria, an early church leader, suggested this.)

In the end, the identity of the Hebrew writer remains a mystery that will only be solved in heaven.

Date and Place

Dates for the writing have been suggested between AD 60 and 70. Most believe it could not have been written later than 70 because the author indicates that the sacrificial system is still being practiced in the temple (Hebrews 8:1-5). This, of course, ended with the destruction of Jerusalem. The fact that he indicates that the system of Judaism as they knew it was soon to pass away (Hebrews 8:13) might lead us to conclude that the letter was written in the late 60s.

Audience

The book was written to Jewish Christians, who were being persecuted and were tempted to return to the relative comfort of Judaism. The author implores them not to go back to their old ways and not to throw away their confidence in Christ.

> So do not throw away your confidence; it will be richly rewarded. You need to persevere so that when you have done the will of God, you will receive what he has promised. (Hebrews 10:35-36)

Purpose

The purpose of the book is twofold.
1. It was written to Jewish Christians, admonishing them not to go back to Judaism.
2. It was written to show the preeminence of Jesus over anything that Judaism had to offer (Hebrews 13:8).

The writer is attempting to show that Jesus is the only way to find God. Judaism would not save. The book of Hebrews is thirteen chapters on one subject. It is the longest sustained argument in the Bible. The writer argues that:

- Jesus is greater than the prophets (Hebrews 1:1-3)
- Jesus is greater than the angels (Hebrews 1:4-2:9)
- Jesus is greater than Moses (Hebrews 3:1-6)
- Jesus is greater than the OT Aaronic priesthood (Hebrews 4:14-10:18)

The writer argues that Jesus is:

- The *archegos* (Hebrews 2:10, 12:2), the Pioneer. He went first and others followed.
- The *prodromos* (Hebrews 6:20), the reconnaissance man who went first to make it safe for others.
- The *mesites* (Hebrews 9:15; 12:24), the mediator, the person who stands in the middle. He stands between God and us, and bringing God to us and us to God.

Characteristics

Hebrews is not a normal letter. It is more like a treatise or tractate. Some say it is a "homiletical Midrash," a Jewish interpretation of Scripture. No other book in the New Testament contains as many OT quotes as Hebrews does. It demonstrates the way the NT writers used the Old Testament. In Hebrews 13:22, the author gives his only identification of what he was writing, calling it a "word of exhortation" (NASB). At various points the author will stop his formal arguments to personally encourage or exhort his readers (for examples, see Hebrews 3:12-4:16; 5:11-6:12; 10:19-39).

Hebrews gives us many practical commandments in chapter 13. Some of these are:

- Christians must always love each other (13:1).
- Hospitality is crucial because some have entertained angels without knowing it (13:2-3).
- Marriage should always be honored and kept pure (13:4).
- Our lives must be free from the love of money and full of contentment. God has never forsaken his people (13:5-6).
- Leadership must be appreciated and imitated (13:7). It should be obeyed (13:17).

- Strange teaching that is not based on grace is to be rejected (13:9).
- God is looking for sacrifices of the heart, which we can now offer to him through Jesus Christ (13:11-16).
- Prayer is vital (13:18-21).

James: A Faith That Works

Authorship

James, the half brother of Jesus, is mentioned in Matthew 13:55; Mark 6:3; Acts 12:17, 15:13, 21:18; 1 Corinthians 15:7; and Galatians 1:19, 2:9, 2:12. James was the younger brother of Jesus and the oldest of eight or nine siblings after Jesus. Although Jesus' family did not accept his role as Messiah at first, his love won them over, including his brother James. In AD 225 the early church leader, Origen, was the first to attribute this book to Jesus' brother James.

Date and Place

James probably should be dated around AD 45-48, making it the first document in the New Testament to be written. This places the letter before the Jerusalem Council and at the zenith of the Jew/Gentile controversy. Why place it here? Because James was a chief player in the Jerusalem Council, logic dictates that he would mention it in his letter if it had already occurred.

James was an elder and pillar of the church in Jerusalem. The book was most likely written there.

Audience

James writes to the "twelve tribes" in the Dispersion (James 1:1), Christian Jews living outside of Palestine. These disciples would have faced the same challenge as those Jews who were taken into exile: the assimilation of pagan culture. James, the most respected of the Jewish Christian leaders along with Peter, writes to those outside of Palestine, warning them of the perils of the world. F. F. Bruce states,

> The Dispersion (*diaspora*) commonly denoted the large number of Jews who lived among the Gentiles outside Palestine—in the Roman provinces to the west or in the Parthian Empire farther east. But the "Dispersion" to which James writes is a Christian dispersion, Jewish-Christian perhaps, but nonetheless certainly Christian.[1]

William Barclay states that James' letter is based on a form of Jewish preaching—the *charaz*—which means "stringing pearls." Barclay states,

> The Jews had their own theories of preaching. One of their main beliefs was that the preacher, in order to maintain the interest of his hearers, must never linger for long on any one subject; he must keep moving quickly and constantly from one subject to another.... So there is little doubt that this letter began life as a Synagogue sermon.[2]

In his letter, James jumps from one topic to another like dropping pearls onto a string to create a pearl necklace.

Purpose

James wrote a synagogue sermon for the Christian Jews outside of Palestine, warning them of the perils of the world. James addresses a number of problems that he sees occurring within the Jewish Christian fellowship of the first century church.

Characteristics

James is one of the most practical books of the New Testament. But throughout the centuries, not everyone has loved the book of James. Martin Luther, the father of the Reformation movement, could not stomach James' teaching on faith and works. James said, "Faith without works is dead" (James 2:26 KJV). Luther felt that faith and works were worlds apart. Therefore, he called James "a right 'strawy' epistle...." He further stated, "I do not hold it to be of apostolic authorship." He placed James in the back of his German Bible—in essence, stripping it from his canon of Scripture. Luther surely misunderstood James' teaching about faith and seemingly missed the fact that "of all the books in the New Testament other than the Four Gospels, this one has the greatest number of parallels to the words of Jesus, particularly to his teaching in the Sermon on the Mount."[3]

1 Peter: Get Ready for Pain

Authorship

The Apostle Peter was the author of 1 Peter.

Date and Place

The letter was written around AD 64-65, at the beginning of Nero's persecution. According to 1 Peter 5:13, Peter was writing from Rome (Babylon), which means that he wrote it not long before he was executed there.

Audience

Peter was writing to various congregations of Asia Minor or modern day Turkey (1 Peter 1:1). The majority of the readers were Gentile Christians (1:14, 18; 2:9-10; 4:3-4).

Purpose

Nero, who became emperor in AD 54, set fire to parts of Rome in AD 64. Ten out of fourteen districts in Rome burned. Nero blamed the Christians for the fire. Didn't Christians teach that the world would end by fire? Why not blame them?

Peter is writing to the churches of northern Galatia, warning them about the persecution in Rome. The shadow of the Empire fell upon north Asia Minor and therefore, persecution was imminent. Peter wanted to ready the churches for it.

Characteristics

Originally, this letter was possibly a sermon. Some believe it was a baptismal sermon (1 Peter 1:23; 2:2) It contains much about how to respond to suffering and calls disciples to follow Jesus' example of submission to others out of reverence for God.

2 Peter; Jude; 1, 2, 3 John
The Peril of Heresies

These five letters were written to cope with heresies (false doctrines) that arose during the second half of the first century. The approach of these letters was positive rather than negative.

The Biblical writers address several types of false teaching. Here are some of them.

- Gnosticism and Docetism
- The Judaizers
- The Libertines
- Those who denied the resurrection (1 Corinthians 15)
- The Nicolaitans

In the early church, several practical measures were taken in order to prevent the rise and spread of false doctrine. False doctrine was looked upon as gangrene that had to be prevented at all costs. Paul, Peter and James called together a council in Jerusalem to prevent the Judaizers from wrecking the church. Several letters were written to combat false doctrine, many of which were often written as a preventative action. Paul made special trips to churches in an attempt to stave off false teachers. He also sent some of his most trusted companions to situations in an attempt to fight false doctrine.

2 Peter

Authorship

2 Peter was written by the apostle Peter.

Date and Place

Liberal scholarship places this letter very late. They cannot envision Peter saying what he said about Paul in 2 Peter 3. They believe that a division grew in the early church over the Jew/Gentile debate. These scholars write that Peter and Paul never agreed on how to treat Gentile converts. They insist that the letter of 2 Peter must have been written in the name of Peter around AD 150.

But there is no reason to believe liberal scholarship here. 2 Peter could very well have been written from Rome before Peter's execution around AD 67-68.

Audience

We are uncertain as to the destination of 2 Peter. It is not unlikely that it was sent to the same audience as the first letter of Peter—various churches in Asia Minor.

Purpose

Peter was writing to protect his readers from heresy. This heresy seems to have involved a denial of the Lordship and redemptive power of Jesus (2 Peter 2:1). He also fights against a complete abandonment of all moral standards and a bold self-assertiveness that accompanied spiritual ignorance (2:10-12).

Jude

Authorship

The book of Jude was written by Jude, the half-brother of Jesus and the brother of James.

Date and Place

This brief book is quite difficult to date. The most likely possibility seems to be around AD 67-68, just before the destruction of the temple in Jerusalem, from Palestine.

Audience

Like his brother James, Jude is associated with the church in Jerusalem. He was writing to Jewish Christians around Palestine.

Purpose

Jude was writing to refute heresy and to encourage Christians to hold to the true faith. What was the heresy that Jude was refuting? It had certain characteristics: (1) it held to a false Christology; (2) it misused the doctrine of grace (the Libertines); and (3) it was a doctrine with a fertile imagination.

1 John

Authorship

John the apostle wrote the letter of 1 John.

Date and Place

The traditional date for the first letter of John is around AD 90-95. Many scholars dated the writings of John late because of his developed Christology, but John could easily be dated in the 70s or 80s. We are not sure of the exact date of this letter. It is easy to just say it was written in the last third of the first century.

If it was written from the Isle of Patmos with the book of Revelation, then it should be given the same date as Revelation—AD 69-79, during the reign of Vespasian.

Audience

John is most likely writing to the disciples of the church in Ephesus, where he labored in the ministry for many years.

Purpose

John was writing against an incipient form of Gnosticism that denied the incarnation of Jesus.

Characteristics

This letter could have served as a sermon that was preached in several churches. John writes about the nature of God that:

- God is light (1 John 1:5). In him is no darkness at all. Light is the symbol of knowledge and purity.
- God is righteous (1 John 2:29). He is all that is right in character and conduct.
- God is love (1 John 4:8).
- God is life (1 John 5:20).

John also gives a series of tests about true Christianity.

- The test of correct belief in Jesus Christ (1 John 2:22-23; 4:2).
- The test of obedience (1 John 2:3-6, 3:10, 5:2). Obedience is the proof of love.
- The test of willingness to listen to the truth (1 John 4:5-6).
- The test of love (1 John 2:9-11, 3:14-18, 4:7-12). Do we love the brothers?
- The test of the possession of God's Spirit (1 John 3:24, 4:13).

2 John

Authorship

John the apostle also wrote 2 John.

Date and Place

Like the first letter of John, this letter was written in the last third of the first century. The place of its origin is uncertain.

Audience

The letter was written to the church—"the elect lady" (2 John 1 RSV).

Purpose

John is writing to protect the church against heresy. In this case he is fighting against Docetism. This word is taken from a Greek word, which means "to seem." They believed that Jesus never took on fleshly form, but only "seemed" to be human.

3 John
Authorship
3 John was also written by the apostle John.

Date and Place
The letter was written during the last third of the first century. The place of writing is unknown.

Audience
John wrote to Gaius, the elder of a church. It was also circulated around the churches of Asia.

Purpose
John wrote because some people were showing a disregard for apostolic authority. Gaius, Diotrephes and Demetrius were the three men mentioned specifically in the letter.

Another issue in the book was hospitality. Some false teachers were taking advantage of the church, so John is writing to stop this practice.

Revelation: The Apocalypse
Authorship
John the apostle wrote the book of Revelation.[4]

Date and Place
Internal evidence suggests that John wrote his revelation during the reign of Vespasian (AD 69-79), although some would argue for a slightly later date, during the reign of Domitian (AD 81-96). I would suggest that Revelation 17:9-11, where we have a reference to eight kings, gives us an important clue as to when Revelation was penned. Here is a list of the Roman emperors of the first century.

- Augustus   27 BC - AD 14
- Tiberius   AD 14-37
- Caligula   AD 37-41
- Claudius   AD 41-54

- Nero   AD 54-68
- Vespasian   AD 69-79[5]
- Titus   AD 79-81
- Domitian   AD 81-96

I would argue that the book was written when the sixth emperor was on the throne—Vespasian AD 69-79—and most likely prophesied about the reign of Domitian.

The book was written from the Isle of Patmos, where John had been sent to live in exile for his beliefs.

Audience

John was writing to the church—specifically, the seven churches of Asia.

Purpose

John was given a vision that probably described what would occur during Domitian's reign (AD 81-96). John is writing to alert the church that troublesome times were right around the corner. He is warning them about the impending persecution that was sure to follow. The basic purpose of the book was to comfort persecuted Christians:

- God sees their tears (Revelation 7:17, 21:4).
- Their prayers move God to act (8:3-4).
- Their deaths are precious in his sight (14:13).
- Their final victory is assured (15:2).
- Their blood will be avenged (6:9-17).
- Christ rules forever (5:11-13).
- Christ is coming again to receive his own (Revelation 21-22).

Characteristics

Revelation was always considered a very difficult book. In the fifth century Jerome (translator of the Vulgate) said that Revelation contained as many secrets as it did words. It is the only NT book on which John Calvin, the great Protestant reformer, did not write a commentary. Martin Luther did not regard it as Scripture at all. He wrote,

> I hold it to be neither apostolic nor prophetic....My spirit cannot acquiesce in the book. I abide by the books, which present Christ as pure and clear....After all, in it Christ is neither taught nor acknowledged.

Zwingli, another Protestant reformer, rejected it by saying, "With the Apocalypse we have no concern, for it is not a Biblical book. The Apocalypse has no savor of the mouth or mind of John. I can, if I so will, reject its testimonies."

Revelation comes from the genre of literature known as apocalyptic literature, which is highly symbolic. Other examples of apocalyptic literature in the Bible include Psalm 18, Isaiah 34 and the books of Ezekiel, Daniel and Zechariah. The symbols in apocalyptic literature tend to be very difficult to understand because they are trying to describe the indescribable and to present a picture of things that no eye has seen, that no ear has heard and that have never entered into the mind of man. They are telling of the unutterable and unimaginable action of God when God enters the world in all his might.

I have a deep conviction that the bulk of the material in the book of Revelation has already been fulfilled. It was written to strengthen Jesus' disciples in the first century. In Revelation 1:3 John mentions that details of his vision would take place soon. We should take him at his word on this. Revelation is not meant to be the "end of time almanac" for Christians. With this misuse of the book, its valuable lessons are often lost in predictions and prognostications about the Second Coming of Jesus.[6] Revelation does give us a dramatic and vivid picture of the victory Jesus will ultimately have over Satan. It can inspire us as it did the early Christians to never give up in the spiritual battle.

Notes

1. F. F. Bruce, *The Message of the New Testament* (Exeter, England: The Paternoster Press, 1972), 90.

2. William Barclay, *A Beginner's Guide to the New Testament* (Edinburgh: Saint Andrew Press, 1976), 21.

3. Bruce Metzger, *The New Testament: Its Background, Growth and Content* (New York: Abingdon Press, 1965), 252.

4. For a more detailed outline of Revelation, see the appendix in my new book *The Final Act* (Woburn, Mass.: DPI, 2000). For a more in-depth treatment of Revelation, see Gordon Ferguson's book *Mine Eyes Have Seen the Glory* (Woburn, Mass.: DPI, 1996).

5. The period of instability that followed Nero's death saw a succession of three men who were declared "emperor" in the space of a year. None, however, gained the allegiance of the entire Roman empire until Vespasian. They were Galba (Oct. 68-Jan 69 AD), Otho (Jan-Mar 69 AD) and Vitellius (June-Dec 69 AD).

6. See *The Final Act* (Woburn, Mass.: DPI, 2000).

Appendixes

Appendix 1
Inspiration and Canonization

Geisler and Nix, in their *A General Introduction to the Bible,* discuss three links in the canonization of Scripture (getting the Bible "from God to us").[1] The first link is inspiration. The second is canonization—the recognition and collection of the prophetic writings. The third link is the transmission of the Bible—the process of copying, translating, recopying and retranslating the Scriptures so that future generations can have the Word.

Inspiration

Two key passages help us understand how the inspiration of the Scriptures came about.

> All scripture is inspired by God and profitable for teaching, for reproof, for correction, for training in righteousness. (2 Timothy 3:16 NASB)

Here the word for "inspired" is *theo-pneustos* ("God-breathed"). The thought is that the Scriptures originate with God.

> No prophecy ever came by the impulse of man, but men moved by the Holy Spirit spoke from God. (2 Peter 1:21 RSV)

Inspiration is the process in which Spirit-inspired writers wrote the God-breathed message. Inspiration is the total process, including writer and writings. Geisler and Nix write,

> The means or process of inspiration is a mystery of the providence of God, but the result of this process is a verbal (the words), plenary (extending to all parts equally), inerrant (errorless), and authoritative record.[2]

There are some things that inspiration did not do:
- Inspiration did not inform when there was no need. In Acts 22:3, Paul already knew the information that is given.
- It did not pretend to make a writer all knowing. In 1 Corinthians 1:16, Paul admitted that he did not remember everyone he baptized. (See also 1 Thessalonians 3:5 and 2 Corinthians 2:12-14.)

- Inspiration did not make a writer sinless. In Galatians 2:11, Paul rebukes Peter for his prejudice against the Gentiles.
- It did not supply the writer with what he could obtain from other sources. Luke 1:1-4 is a key passage on the writer's use of sources. In Acts 20:6 and 20:13, Luke kept an inspired travel diary.

We must not confuse the *process* with the *product*. The process could involve heathen sources, man's limited knowledge or gifted arguments. The writers kept their personalities. They were not God's typewriters. But the end product is inspired.

Basic Views of Inspiration

1. *Liberal View:* The Bible *contains* the word of God, but it is not synonymous with it. Liberal scholars say the Bible is not the complete word of God. Man must discern God's word within the Bible. This is based on naturalism and rationalism. This view is man-centered.

2. *Neoorthodox View* (Karl Barth and Rudolf Bultmann): a movement made prominent in the early 1900s that proposed that the Bible *becomes* the word of God. When God chooses to use the imperfect channel to better man, then the Bible is speaking truth. These scholars would say that there is no objective truth. Instead, truth is different for everyone. This is a subjective approach.

   Rudolf Bultmann and others strove to demythologize the Bible— to strip culture out of the Bible to get at the core of truth. They believed the Bible was the product of the church and that not every saying attributed to Jesus came from Jesus. They believed that some of the portrait of Jesus was invented by the church. It becomes the goal of the Bible student to strip the church's view out of the Bible.

3. *Conservative View:* The Bible is the word of God, but is the product of verbal dictation (divine teletype). The writers were secretaries, copying every word that God directly gave them. This does not account for differences in vocabulary and thought.

4. *Dynamic View* adherents believe in thought inspiration. God supplied the thoughts and nothing else. This goes too far to the other extreme.

5. *Biblical View* : The writers received thought inspiration, and yet God did at times give exact words. God also gave the writers the freedom

to write in their own styles. Each word in the Bible is God-breathed. He watched over the process so that the final product was inspired. The end product is as accurate as if God had mechanically dictated it word for word, yet it is writer-oriented, as if the writer had the freedom to compose it. This is the wonder and glory of Biblical inspiration.

The Bible Claims to Be an Inspired Book

- The classic text on inspiration is 2 Timothy 3:16.
- Paul spoke in "words taught by the Spirit" (1 Corinthians 2:13).
- Jesus indicated that not even the smallest part of a Hebrew word or letter could be destroyed (Matthew 5:18).
- The New Testament refers to the written record as the "oracles of God" (Romans 3:2, Hebrews 5:12 KJV).
- Jesus said, "Scripture cannot be broken" (John 10:35).
- Paul's writings were accepted very early as Scripture (2 Peter 3:15-16).
- The Bible states that no prophetic utterance ever came about by any means other than the Holy Spirit (2 Peter 1:20-21).
- Jesus promised to give his disciples a Spirit-directed ministry (John 14:26, 16:13).
- The New Testament church claimed to have a prophetic gift (cf. Ephesians 4:11, 1 Corinthians 14:31-32).
- Under one phrase, "for the Scripture says," 1 Timothy 5:18 quotes from Luke 10:7 and Deuteronomy 25:4. Here the writings of Luke, who was not an apostle, were accepted as Scripture on the same level as the writings from Deuteronomy.

Evidences for Inspiration

Argument from the Dynamic Ability of the Bible

The Bible transforms lives. It has changed society and individuals within society.

Argument from the Integrity of Jesus

Geisler and Nix write, "Since Jesus' veracity is unquestionable, it remains only to discover what he taught with authority about the Bible. He considered Scripture the 'unbreakable Word of God.'"[3]

Argument from the Unity of the Bible

Geisler and Nix state,

> The Bible contains hundreds of themes, written in several languages, by nearly forty writers, over a period of about fifteen hundred years, in several different countries, by people of various occupations. Yet, amid all this diversity there is a sustained unity of subject, teaching, and solution to man's problem of sin.[4]

Argument from the Prophecies of the Bible

Passages of Scripture have repeatedly foretold the future.
- The destruction of Tyre (Ezekiel 26)
- The prediction of the world's great kingdoms (Daniel 2 and 7)
- The coming of the Messiah (Daniel 9:24-27)

Argument from the Historicity of the Bible

Archaeology continues to substantiate the Scriptures.

Good Book or God's Book?

Geisler and Nix write:

> It must be remembered that the Bible repeatedly claims to be God's Word, and it would be morally incongruous for the very book that presents the highest morality to be itself the perpetrator of one of the world's biggest lies, namely, that it is God's Word, when in actuality it is not. If it be suggested that the writers wrongly attributed it to God, then their integrity, or authority to speak on morality, is undermined, and there is not reasonable explanation left for the Bible's superiority.[5]

Charles Wesley writes:

> The Bible must be the invention either of good men or angels, bad men or devils, or of God.
> 1. It could not be the invention of good men or angels; for they neither would or could make a book, and tell lies all the time they were writing it saying, 'Thus says the Lord,' when it was their own invention.
> 2. It could not be the invention of bad men or devils; for they would not make a book which commands all duty, forbids all sin, and condemns their souls to hell to all eternity.

3. Therefore, I draw this conclusion, that the Bible must be given by divine inspiration.

Canonicity

Canonization tells how the Bible received its acceptance. A *kanon* was a rod, ruler, staff or measuring rod. It came to mean a "standard or norm." A book became a part of the canon because it was inspired. Edward J. Young, an OT scholar, writes,

> When the Word of God was written it became Scripture and, inasmuch as it had been spoken by God, possessed absolute authority. Since it was the Word of God, it was canonical. That which determines the canonicity of a book, therefore, is the fact that the book is inspired by God.[6]

Here are some scriptures that help explain the process of canonization.

- John 16:13—Jesus promised that the Holy Spirit would guide the apostles into "all truth." This implies that the truth would be revealed to the apostles; therefore, we can accept apostolic teaching as truth. It also demonstrates that the Holy Spirit would guide the process of inspiration and canonization.
- John 14:26—Jesus promises the apostles that the Holy Spirit would bring all things that he had taught them to their remembrance. This shows that Jesus was looking over and guarding the process of inspiration.
- 1 John 4:1-6—The apostle John strongly urged that "truth" be tested by the known standard before it was received. John gave the early church authority to test the spirits. He gave them authority to determine truth. The early church had the authority to determine which scriptures were inspired. God inspired the book; the church tested it and recognized its inspiration. Some books were not received into the canon until the second century (2 Peter and Revelation), but they ultimately passed the test of inspiration.
- Acts 2:42—The church continued in the "apostles' teaching." Apostolic authority was very important in the first century. Geisler and Nix comment here:

> The term 'apostolic' as used for the test of Canonicity does not necessarily mean 'apostolic authorship,' or 'that which was prepared

under the direction of the Apostles,' unless the word 'apostle' be taken in its nontechnical sense, meaning someone beyond the twelve apostles or Paul. In this non-technical sense, Barnabas is called an apostle (Acts 14:14), as is James (Galatians 1:19), and evidently others too (Romans 16:7; 2 Corinthians 8:23; Philippians 2:25). ...In fact, the writer of Hebrews disclaims being an apostle, saying that the message of Christ 'was attested to us [readers and writer] by those [the apostles] who heard him' (Hebrews 2:3). ...it is apostolic authority, or apostolic approval, that was the primary test for Canonicity, and not merely apostolic authorship.[7]

- 2 Peter 3:15-16—Peter speaks of "all his [Paul's] letters" being on a level with "the other Scriptures." By the time of 2 Peter in AD 66, Paul's epistles were considered a part of the canon.
- 1 Thessalonians 5:21—Paul commands the church to "test everything." This is especially within the context of prophecy. Paul gave the early church authority to test prophecy and see what really came from God. This is a canonistic test.

Factors Which Led to the Development of the Canon

- Inadequacy of the Old Testament
- Decline of oral tradition and the demise of eyewitnesses: after the apostles left the scene, their writing was seen as valuable. Since it was valuable, it should be preserved.
- Demands of the early church: the early church wanted to know which books should be read in worship and which books should be circulated as Scripture.
- Rise of heresy:
    1. Gnosticism: Claimed their books were as inspired as the Gospels
    2. Marcionism: Marcion lived in 145 and was a Christian at Rome. He had a canon of eleven books, a revised book of Luke and eleven of Paul's epistles.
- Presence of many types of Christian writings
- Use of the Codex (= "book"): Developed between 175-200, the scrolls were placed in book form for convenience. Scholars are finding new evidence which suggests that the Codex was being used in the first century AD.

- Persecution: The Diocletian persecution in 302/303-305 delivered an edict to kill Christians and destroy their books. Eusebius records,

  ...an imperial letter was everywhere promulgated, ordering the razing of the churches to the ground and the destruction by fire of the Scriptures, and proclaiming that those who held high positions would lose all civil rights, while those in households, if they persisted in their profession of Christianity, would be deprived of their liberty.

- Official publication of the New Testament: Constantine authorized Eusebius to make fifty copies of the New Testament. This signaled the completion of the canon. In Eusebius' history we find a letter, *Victor Constantinus, Maximus Augustus, to Eusebius,* which reads,

  ...I have thought it expedient to instruct your Prudence to order fifty copies of the sacred Scriptures, the provision and use of which you know to be most needful for the instruction of the Church, to be written on prepared parchment in a legible manner, and in a convenient, portable form, by professional transcribers thoroughly practiced in their art.

  This letter dates from AD 330. In the same century the church began to give official recognition to the twenty-seven books of the New Testament (AD 363 at Laodicea and AD 397 at Carthage).

- Missionary stimulus: As the gospel was taken to other countries, a need arose to translate the Scriptures into new languages. This meant a canon needed to be recognized so it could be translated.
- Implications for the canon in the New Testament:

  I charge you before the Lord to have this letter read to all the brothers. (1 Thessalonians 5:27)

  After this letter has been read to you, see that it is also read in the church of the Laodiceans and that you in turn read the letter from Laodicea. (Colossians 4:16)

  Until I come, devote yourself to the public reading of Scripture, to preaching and to teaching. (1 Timothy 4:13)

Blessed is the one who reads the words of this prophecy, and blessed are those who hear it and take to heart what is written in it, because the time is near. (Revelation 1:3)

"He who has an ear, let him hear what the Spirit says to the churches. To him who overcomes, I will give the right to eat from the tree of life, which is in the paradise of God." (Revelation 2:7)

"He who has an ear, let him hear what the Spirit says to the churches. He who overcomes will not be hurt at all by the second death." (Revelation 3:6, 13, 22)

"He who has an ear, let him hear what the Spirit says to the churches. To him who overcomes, I will give some of the hidden manna. I will also give him a white stone with a new name written on it, known only to him who receives it." (Revelation 2:17)

"He who has an ear, let him hear what the Spirit says to the churches." (Revelation 2:29, 3:6, 13, 22)

Principles of Canonicity
- Apostolic Testimony: Was it written by an apostle or someone closely associated with an apostle?
- Antiquity: How old is the book? The closer to the apostles, the better. The apocryphal book, *The Shepherd of Hermas,* was excluded from the canon because it is too distant from the leaders of the early church.
- Orthodoxy: Is it orthodox or a heresy? The Marcion books were full of heresy, so they were excluded.
- Reception by the Churches: A book received by the brotherhood was accepted.
- Spiritual Value: What spiritual value did it have?

The History of the Canon
Initial Collections (AD 90-180)
The books of Paul as Scripture (2 Peter 3:16-17) are referred to around AD 66. If Jude quoted from Peter's writing when he said, "you must remember,

beloved, the predictions of the apostles of our Lord Jesus Christ" (v17 RSV), then he not only verified that Peter's writing was accepted into the canon by that time, but that the books received were immediately and authoritatively quoted as Scripture.

Here are some of the early collections of the Biblical books:

- Papias—AD 130. He knew the gospels of Matthew and Mark.
- Justin Martyr—AD 140. He quotes from all the Gospels, most of Paul's epistles, 1 Peter and Revelation.
- Polycarp—AD 150. The disciple of the apostle John. Polycarp quotes from Matthew, John, the first ten of Paul's epistles, 1 Peter, and 1 and 2 John.
- Justin—AD 155. He spoke of the "memories of the apostles."
- Marcion—AD 160. He knew the gospel of Luke. He was the first to develop a canon.
- Tatian—AD 170. He knew the four Gospels. They were collected in the *Diatessaron,* which means "through the four."

Emergence of the Canon (AD 180-220)

During the years AD 180-220, four collections of Biblical books emerged. These were:

- The Muratorian Canon—AD 170. This collection had all the books except Hebrews, James and 1 and 2 Peter. The Muratorian fragment is the earliest canonical list aside from Marcion's canon.
- Irenaeus—AD 170. The first early church father who himself quoted almost every book of the New Testament. He quoted or considered as authentic twenty-three of the twenty-seven books, omitting only Philemon, James, 2 Peter and 3 John.
- Clement of Alexandria—AD 200. Clement collected a canon of twenty-four books. He omitted 2 Timothy, and 2 and 3 John.
- Tertullian—AD 200 He omitted James, 2 Peter, and 2 and 3 John.

Other collections began to emerge during this time. For example:

- The Old Syriac—Circulated in Syria about AD 400, but represented a text dating from the end of the second century. It included all of the twenty-seven New Testament books except 2 Peter, 2 and 3 John, Jude and Revelation.

- The Old Latin—Translated prior to AD 200 and served as the Bible of the Western church. Contains all the NT books except Hebrews, James, and 1 and 2 Peter.
- Codex Barococcis—AD 206. This list proved to include sixty-four of the familiar sixty-six books of the English Bible. Only Esther and Revelation were omitted.

The Fixation of the Canon (AD 220-400)

Several important characters emerged on the scene of the early church to pull together the canon that we use today.

- Origen—AD 225. He divided the books into different categories: (1) accepted, (2) disputed, (3) rejected. He had a thirty-book canon.
- Eusebius, the early church historian—AD 325

1. He described as universally accepted into the canon: the four Gospels, Acts, the thirteen letters of Paul, Hebrews, 1 John, 1 Peter and Revelation.

2. He described these as accepted by the majority: James, 2 Peter, 2 and 3 John and Jude.

3. He spoke of as spurious—the *Didache, The Gospel of Barnabas, The Shepherd of Hermis, The Gospel to the Hebrews, The Acts of Paul* and *The Apocalypse of Peter.*

- Athanasius—AD 367. Athanasius is known as "the father of orthodoxy." He clearly and emphatically listed all twenty-seven books as canonical, saying:

  Again it is not tedious to speak of the books of the New Testament. These are, the four gospels, according to Matthew, Mark, Luke, and John. Afterwards, the Acts of the Apostles and Epistles (called Catholic), seven, namely, of James, one; of Peter, two; of John, three; after these, one of Jude. In addition, there are fourteen Epistles of Paul, written in this order: the first, to the Romans; then, two to the Corinthians; after these, to the Galatians; next, to the Ephesians; then to the Philippians; then to the Colossians; after these, two to the Thessalonians, and then, to the Hebrews; and again, two to Timothy; one to Titus; and lastly, that to Philemon. And besides, the Revelation of John.

- Jerome and Augustine—AD 400. both accepted our canon of twenty-seven books.

- The councils of Hippo (AD 393) and Carthage (AD 397) ratified the present-day canon of the twenty-seven books of the New Testament.
- The *Antilegomena* (meaning "spoken against") numbered seven books.

Why were the disputed book questioned? Here are some answers.
- Hebrews: This was questioned because of its anonymity.
- James: This was questioned as to its veracity. The supposed conflict with Paul's teaching on grace hurt its acceptance.
- 2 Peter: Its genuineness was questioned. Also, its dissimilarity to 1 Peter brought questions.
- 2 and 3 John: These were questioned as to their genuineness. The author identified himself not as an apostle, but as an elder.
- Jude: This was disputed on the question of authenticity mainly because it quoted an apocryphal book, the *Book of Enoch*.
- Revelation: Its authenticity was challenged. A controversy over millennialism arose because of this book.

Transmission—The Rise and Growth of the New Testament

Ancient books were made from two types of material.
1. Papyrus—A triangular reed found in the Nile delta. It grows twelve to fifteen feet high and was cut into pieces around one foot long. These were cut into strips and crossed together to weave sheets. The rosin in the reeds held the strips together. Papyrus was used until the fourth century AD.
2. Vellum—this is the skin of a goat, calf or sheep. The skin was boiled, bleached and chalked to make it white. It was sometimes referred to as parchment. This was used from the fourth to the thirteenth centuries.

Ancient books were collected in two forms.
1. Scrolls—The earliest type of manuscript. About twelve inches high and thirty to thirty-six feet long. Most of these were made of parchment.
2. Codices—a Codex. Historians believe the Codex came from early Christian endeavors to preserve their manuscripts. This is book form.

Early Christian documents have been discovered that used three modes of writing.

1. Majuscule, also called Uncial—first through ninth centuries. Capital letters without a break.
2. Cursive—Some first century writing was cursive. This style was popular for personal notes, not for formal writing.
3. Minuscule—eighth century and following. This means small letters.

Scholars have collected thousands of manuscripts relating to the early transmission of the text. Of these manuscripts, they have catalogued:

- Papyrus
- Majuscules
- Minuscules—2,792
- Lectionaries—2,193 (a text of Scripture spread out over the year for the church)
- More than 5,000 fragments behind our text (in the Greek)
- More than 40,000 manuscripts in all languages

How Did the Early Scribes Copy the Manuscripts?

Down to the fourth century AD, the manuscripts were copied one by one—by a single copyist. These copyists took great care. They did not allow errors to remain in the copies. If an error was discovered, the whole copy was destroyed and a new one was begun.

In the fourth century the Emperor Constantine made Christianity the official religion of the Roman empire. A place called the "Scriptorium" was formed. In the Scriptorium a reader read the scripture and the copyists listened and wrote from dictation. These men were paid for the number of manuscripts they copied, so they did not care for accuracy. The copies of the text were corrupted during this time.

In the Byzantine period, the fifth and sixth centuries, the monks took over the task of copying the Scriptures. They returned to the tradition of the earlier copyists, taking great pains to ensure that each copy was correct. Charles Pellegrino, in his *Return to Sodom and Gomorrah,* comments about the scribes who copied the Dead Sea Scrolls:

> The Qumran texts are almost a thousand years older than the Aleppo Codex, which was written in Israel about AD 900 and was, until AD 1947, the oldest-known Hebrew manuscript containing the full text of the Bible. What has surprised most scholars is that in spite of the millennium of hand copying that separates them, the Aleppo Codex and the books of the Old

Testament unearthed at Qumran are virtually identical. One of the oldest of the Dead Sea Scrolls, dating to about 200 BC, is the Book of Isaiah. Only thirteen minor variations from the Aleppo text and from its modern descendants have been identified. If this assumption is correct, then the modern Hebrew Bible is, in most essentials, the same Bible one would have found in Babylon in 550 BC.[8]

This attestation shows how careful the scribes of the Bible were to transmit exactly what the text said. The text of the Bible has been carefully handed down from generation to generation through the centuries.

The Greek Bible that scholars use today to translate the Scriptures into different languages has been edited together from several thousand manuscripts with hundreds of variant readings. Most of these variants are small and inconsequential. When the scholars must make decisions as to which variants to include in the text, they rely heavily on certain text types and manuscripts that are considered to be more reliable. Some of these reliable manuscripts are listed in the following:

The Most Important Papyri

- p52—John Rylands' papyrus[9]—is the oldest New Testament text we have. Found in 1920, it fits in the palm of your hand. It has been dated to AD 115-125.
- p45, p46, p47—These are the oldest consecutive texts of the four Gospels and Paul's epistles, are dated at around AD 200 and are known as the Chester Beatty papyri.
- p66, p75—Bodmer papyri are dated around AD 200.

The Most Important Uncials

- "B"—Vaticanus Codex is the oldest complete New Testament manuscript.
- "Aleph"—Codex Sinaiticus contains almost all of the Old Testament and all of the New Testament. This manuscript dates from the early fourth century, around AD 325-350. Count Tischendorf, a Russian, discovered it in a monastery at the base of Mt. Sinai in 1859. The monks of the monastery were using the pages of this manuscript to start fires. The British Museum bought this codex from Russia in 1933 for 100,000 pounds. It is currently in the British Museum.

- "A"—Codex Alexandrinus contains all of books of the Old and New Testaments. This text, which dates to the fifth century, was found in Alexandria, Egypt.

The Apocrypha

The canon of the Catholic church and other Orthodox churches is different from the Protestant Bible in that it contains several books from the intertestamental period—the time between the close of the Old Testament and the beginning of the New Testament. These books are called the Apocrypha. Why are these books not in the Protestant Bible? The are several reasons for the rejection of the Apocrypha into the canon.

- These books were never included in the Hebrew canon. The Jews did not accept them as Scripture.
- Josephus expressly excludes them.
- Philo, the Jewish philosopher in Alexandria (c. 20 BC-AD 50) quoted the Old Testament very frequently, yet never quoted the Apocrypha, nor even mentioned these books.
- Targums (Aramaic paraphrases) were provided for the canonical books but were not provided for the Apocrypha.
- These books are never quoted in the New Testament. Most of the apocryphal material existed and was likely incorporated into Septuagint editions in the New Testament period, yet it is never cited by Jesus or the apostles. New Testament references, rather, allude to the commonly accepted Hebrew canon. The use of "Scripture" in the New Testament represents such an allusion (compare 2 Timothy 3:16). Jesus appeals to the strict Hebrew canon in Matthew 23:35 and Luke 24:45.
- Christian tradition offers no real support for accepting the Apocrypha as canonical.
- These books are not included in the canonical lists of the early centuries.
- Jerome expressly supported the strict Hebrew canon and emphatically rejected the Apocrypha as secondary.
- Books of the Apocrypha were considered suitable for reading and instruction, but they were not considered authoritative in the early centuries.

- The Apocrypha was first declared canonical by the reactionary Roman Catholic Council of Trent (AD 1546). This councilor decision was transparently dogmatic. A narrow majority passed this action. The council then anathematized all who might disagree.
- The Apocrypha bears no internal marks of inspiration.
- No writer of any of the books of the Apocrypha actually claims inspiration; indeed, some disclaim it.
- These books contain historical, geographical and chronological errors.
- Doctrinally, the books at times contradict the canonical Scriptures.
- Stylistically, the books are inferior to the canonical Scriptures.
- Stories in the Apocrypha contain some legendary and fantastic material.
- Their moral and spiritual level is beneath that of the canonical Scriptures.
- Proper dating of the Apocrypha shows its noncanonical character.
- These books were written later than those of the Old Testament were.
- Portions of these books even date from the Christian era, perhaps as interpolations.

These books of the Apocrypha form no part of the canon, but rather serve as witnesses to life and thought in the intertestamental period.

Notes

1. Norman Geisler and William E. Nix, *A General Introduction to the Bible* (Chicago: Moody Press, 1980), 148-149.

2. Ibid., 36.

3. Ibid., 117.

4. Ibid., 118.

5. Ibid., 121.

6. Edward J. Young. An Introduction to the Old Testament (Grand Rapids, Mich.: Wm. B. Eerdmans, 1994), 86.

7. Geiser and Nix, 91-92.

8. Charles Pellegrino, *Return to Sodom and Gomorrah* (New York: Random House, 1994), 254.

9. The initial "p" refers to "papyrus."

Appendix 2
Tools for Bible Study

The place to start building a Bible library is with the catalog of books produced by DPI (Discipleship Publications International) and GCI (Great Commission Illustrated). Their books are practical and Biblically oriented— and are written or produced by disciples. Every disciple of Christ Jesus should become familiar with these books. Here is a list of other books that will strengthen Bible study.

Translations

American Standard Version (1901)—the best literal translation
New American Standard Bible (1962)—A more readable revision of the ASV
Revised Standard Version (1952—a great thought-for-thought translation
New Revised Standard Version (1989)—A more readable revision of the RSV
New International Version (1978)—a most readable English translation
The Jerusalem Bible—a great comparative translation
The Poet's Bible—by David Rosenberg, a wonderful translation of many of the Old Testament poetic texts
A Harmony of the Gospels—by A. T. Robinson
The Message—a paraphrase, using common, everyday language

A wide variety of complete translations can now be accessed on the Internet. To locate these just enter the translation name into a search engine.

Study Bibles

An important tool for every Bible student is a good analytical study Bible.

The Harper's Study Bible
The Thompson Chain Reference Bible
The Oxford Study Bible

Concordances

An exhaustive concordance is a necessary tool. For the New International Version, use the *NIV Exhaustive Concordance* published by Zondervan. Software versions of concordances offer the Bible student greater speed, convenience and additional features. "QuickVerse" from Parsons Technology and "WordSearch" from NavPress are among the more popular editions.

History of the Biblical Text

The Text of the New Testament—Bruce Metzger*
How We Got the Bible—Neil Lightfoot#

Bible Handbooks

These are good introductory tools for the general Bible student.

Eerdman's Handbook to the Bible
Abingdon's Bible Study Handbook

Bible Dictionaries

New Bible Dictionary—ed. by J. D. Douglas
The International Standard Bible Encyclopedia, 5 Vols.*
Harper's Bible Dictionary—ed. by Achtemeier

Word Studies

New International Dictionary of New Testament Theology, 3 Vols.*
Theological Wordbook of the Old Testament, 2 Vols.*
New Testament Words—William Barclay#

Atlases

Oxford Bible Atlas
Rand McNally Bible Atlas
The Harper Atlas of the Bible

Archaeology

The Biblical World—Charles Pfeiffer
The Ancient Near East in Pictures—Pritchard*
Light from the Ancient Past—Finegan

Old Testament Background

The History of Israel—John Bright*
Old Testament History—Charles Pfeiffer*
A Survey of the Old Testament Introduction—Gleason Archer

Introduction to the Old Testament—R. K. Harrison
Understanding the Old Testament—Bernhard W. Anderson*
God with Us—Christoph Barth*

Old Testament Commentaries

The New Bible Commentary: Revised, 1 Vol.
Tyndale Old Testament Commentaries
The Daily Bible Study Series
The Living Word Commentaries
Word Biblical Commentaries

New Testament Background

New Testament Times—Merrill C. Tenney
The New Testament Era—Bo Reicke
The New Testament Environment—Eduard Lohse
Introduction to the New Testament—H. C. Thiessen*
New Testament Introduction—Donald Guthrie*
Between the Testaments—D. S. Russell*
New Testament Survey—Merrill C. Tenny
Introducing the New Testament—John Drane

New Testament Commentaries

Tyndale New Testament Commentaries
The New International Commentaries
The Living Word Commentaries
The Daily Bible Study Series—William Barclay
*The New International Greek Commentaries**

Church History

Eerdman's Handbook to the History of Christianity—ed. by Tim Dowley
Pilgrims in Their Own Land—Martin E. Marty
The Spreading Fire—F. F. Bruce
Prepared to Answer—Gordon Ferguson
Nelson's Quick Reference Introduction to Church History—ed. by Howard F. Vos
A New Eusebius—ed. by J. Stevenson
How to Read Church History, Vols. I-II—Jean Comby

Christian Evidences

How Should We Then Live?—Francis A. Schaeffer
The God Who Is There—Francis A. Schaeffer
He Is There and He Is Not Silent—Francis A. Schaeffer
Evidence That Demands a Verdict—Josh McDowell
Protestant Christian Evidences—Bernard Ramm

Devotional Books

Celebration of Discipline—Richard Foster
The Screwtape Letters—C. S. Lewis
Mere Christianity—C. S. Lewis
The Cost of Discipleship—D. Bonhoeffer
Purity of Heart Is to Will One Thing—Soren Kierkegaard
Prayer—M. Quoist
The New Oxford Book of Christian Verse
Leaves from the Notebook of a Tamed Critic—Reinhold Niebuhr
The Singer Trilogy—Calvin Miller
The Spirit of the Disciplines—Dallas Willard
Certain Trumpets—Gary Wills
Prayer: The Cry of the Kingdom—Stanley J. Grenz
Peculiar Treasures—Frederick Buechner

Notes

\# = "for the beginner"
* = "for deeper study"

Appendix 3
Reading the Bible

Use this calendar to read through the Bible in a year.

January	*February*	*March*	*April*
1-2 Peter	1-3 John	1-2 Corinthians	1-2 Timothy
Mark	John	Titus	Philemon
Isaiah	Jeremiah	Ezekiel	Daniel
Numbers	Lamentations	Joshua	Hosea
Judges	1-2 Samuel	Leviticus	Ruth

May	*June*	*July*	*August*
Luke	Acts	Galatians	Colossians
Proverbs	Ecclesiastes	Ephesians	1-2 Thessalonians
Genesis	Song of Songs	Joel	Habakkuk
Exodus	Deuteronomy	Zephaniah	Job
		Psalms 51-100	1 Chronicles
		Malachi	Nahum

September	*October*	*November*	*December*
Romans	Matthew	Hebrews	Philippians
James	Jude	Revelation	Amos
Esther	Ezra	2 Chronicles	Haggai
Nehemiah	Psalms 101-150	Obadiah	Micah
Jonah	Zechariah	Psalms 1-50	
2 Kings	1 Kings		

Appendix 4
One Hundred Useful Passages

The Bible is a tool that can be used to teach other people about God. But to use it, we must be familiar with the book. This list will help you locate useful passages in the Bible. Learn to locate the following useful passages by chapter number only. Verse references and verse memorization are unnecessary. Begin using these passages as soon as possible in your Bible studies.[1]

Matthew

1:25	Mary's virginity (Catholicism)
6:15	Forgiveness in damaged relationships
6:33-34	Seeking first the kingdom
7:7-11	Seeking and finding
7:13-14	Narrow road
13:55-56	Jesus' family (Catholicism)
18:15-17	Church discipline
22:29	Biblical ignorance
23:9	Honorific titles ("Father")
28:19-20	Great Commission

Mark

1:16-20	Fishers of men
2:22	Fresh start (wineskins)
3:20-21	Family opposition
7:6-9	Traditions
7:20-23	Sin
11:24	Faith
16:16	Baptism

Luke

6:22-23, 26	Opposition—when opposed, leap for joy
9:23-26, 9:57-62	Discipleship
10:38-42	Worry and distraction—Mary and Martha
13:1-5	Repentance

14:25-34	Counting the cost
16:13	Two masters (see also 14:26)
18:9-14	Self-righteousness—Pharisee and tax collector

John

1:14	Incarnation
2:17	Jesus' zeal and conviction
4:23-24	True worship
12:24	Death to self
12:47-49	Word
13:34-35	Discipleship (love)
14:6-7	Jesus, the way to the Father
15:8, 16	Discipleship (fruit)
17:20-21	Prayer for unity

Acts

2:6-11	Speaking in tongues
2:38	Conversion
2:42-47	New Testament church
8:17	Spiritual gifts and the laying on of hands
11:26	Disciples called Christians
17:10-12	Bereans
22:16	Baptism
24:25	Convenience
26:19-21	Repentance

Romans

1:18-32	Sin; the Fall
3:23-24	Sin
6:3-4	Baptism
6:23	Sin
8:9	Spirit
13:8	Debt
16:17	Divisive people

1 Corinthians

| 1:10-12 | Factions (denominations) |
| 4:3-4 | Motives and conscience |

2 Thessalonians
3:10   Get a job!

1 Timothy
2:5   One mediator
4:1-5   Celibacy and food rules
4:16   Word

2 Timothy
1:7   Spirit
2:15   Workman (the Word)
2:23-26   Patient instruction
3:1-5   Sin
3:16-17   Word
4:1-5   Preach the Word!

Titus
1:5-9   Eldership (also 1 Timothy 3)
2:11   Grace

Philemon
(All)   Leadership style

Hebrews
3:12-13   Church
4:12-13   Word
5:11-14   Spiritual maturity
10:23-25   Church
11:6   Faith
12:14-17   Bitter root
13:4   Premarital sex
13:7, 17   Leadership

James
1:19-21, 26   Quick to listen; control tongue
2:24   "Faith alone"?

| 4:17 | Sins of omission |
| 5:16 | Confession |

1 Peter

2:21-25	Cross
3:1-7	Marriage
3:21	Baptism
4:3-4	Partying

2 Peter

1:3-11	Spiritual growth
2:1-3	False prophets
2:20-22	Falling away
3:16	Paul's writings as Scripture

1 John

2:3-6	Obedience
2:15-17	Worldliness
4:20	Hatred and racism
5:13	Assurance of salvation

Revelation

3:16	Lukewarmness
3:20	Knocking at the door
21:8	Sin
22:18-19	Word

Note

1. I believe that I first saw this list in a class taught by my good friend and fellow kingdom teacher, Dr. Douglas Jacoby. I have amended the list over the years. Thanks to Douglas for introducing me to this list.

Bibliography

Aharoni, Yohanan. *The Land of the Bible: A Historical Geography.* Philadelphia: Westminster Press, 1979.

———— and Michael Avi-Yonah. *The Macmillan Bible Atlas.* New York: Macmillan, 1977.

Archer, Gleason L. *The Encyclopedia of Bible Difficulties.* Grand Rapids: Zondervan, 1982.

Barnett, Paul. *Is the New Testament History?* Ann Arbor, Mich.: Vine, 1986.

Barr, James. *The Bible and the Modern World.* New York: Harper & Row, 1973.

Beasley, James R., et al. *An Introduction to the Bible.* Nashville: Abingdon Press, 1991.

Berkhof, L. *Principles of Bible Interpretation.* Grand Rapids, Michigan: Baker Book House, 1962.

Blackman, E. C. *Biblical Interpretation.* Philadelphia: The Westminster Press, 1957.

Bloomberg, Craig. *The Historical Reliability of the Gospels.* Downers Grove, Ill.: InterVarsity Press, 1987.

Boyd, Gregory A. *Cynic, Sage or Son of God? Recovering the Real Jesus in an Age of Revisionist Replies.* Wheaton, Ill.: BridgePoint, 1995.

Brown, Robert. *The Bible Speaks to You.* Philadelphia: The Westminster Press, 1955.

Bruce, F. F. *The New Testament Documents: Are They Reliable?* Grand Rapids: Wm. B. Eerdmans, 1960.

Drane, John. *Introducing the New Testament.* San Francisco: Harper & Row, 1986.

Drumwright, H. L., Jr. "Interpretation." In *The Zondervan Pictorial Encyclopedia of the Bible.* Edited by Merrill C. Tenney. Vol. III. Grand Rapids: Zondervan, 1975.

Dugan, D. R. *Hermeneutics.* Cincinnati: The Standard Publishing Company, [n.d.].

Finegan, Jack. *The Archaeology of the New Testament.* Princeton: Princeton University Press, 1992.

Ferguson, Everett. *Backgrounds of Early Christianity.* Grand Rapids: Wm. B. Eerdmans, 1989.

Frank, Harry Thomas. *Discovering the Biblical World*. Maplewood: Hammond, 1988.

Geisler, Norman L. and Thomas Howe. *When Critics Ask*. Wheaton, Ill.: Victor, 1992.

_____ and William E. Nix. *A General Introduction to the Bible*. Chicago: Moody Press, 1980.

Grobel, K. "Interpretation." In *The Interpreter's Bible Dictionary*. Edited by George Buttrick. Vol. III. Nashville: Abingdon, 1965.

Johnson, Alan. "History and Culture in New Testament Interpretation." In *Interpreting the Word of God*. Edited by Samuel J. Schultz and Morris A. Inch. Chicago: Moody Press, 1967

Kenyan, Frederic. *Handbook to the Textual Criticism of the New Testament*. New York: Macmillan, 1912.

Machen, J. Gresham. *What is Faith?* Grand Rapids, Mich.: Wm. B. Eerdmans Publishing Company, 1962.

Maier, Gerhard. *The End of the Historical-Critical Method*. St. Louis: Concordia Publishing House, 1974.

Metzger, Bruce M. *The Canon of the New Testament*. Oxford: Clarendon Press, 1988.

_____. *The Text of the New Testament*. Oxford: Oxford University Press, 1992.

Mickelson, A. Berkeley. *Interpreting the Bible*. Grand Rapids: Wm. B. Eerdmans Publishing Company, 1963.

Miller, J. Maxwell. *Introducing the Holy Land: A Guidebook for First-Time Visitors*. Macon, Ga.: Mercer University Press, 1982.

Morison, Frank. *Who Moved the Stone?* Grand Rapids: Zondervan, 1987.

Murphy-O'Connor, Jerome. *The Holy Land: An Archaeological Guide from Earliest Times to 1700*. 3rd ed. New York: Oxford University Press, 1992.

Pritchard, James B. *The Harper Atlas of the Bible*. New York: Harper & Row, 1987.

Ramm, Bernard. *Protestant Biblical Interpretation*. Boston: W. A. Wilde Company, 1956.

Schodde, G. H. "Interpretation." In *The International Standard Bible Encyclopedia*. Edited by James Orr. Vol. III. Grand Rapids: Wm. B. Eerdmans, 1979.

Smart, James D. *The Interpretation of Scripture.* Philadelphia: The Westminster Press, 1961.

Sterrett, T. Norton. *How to Understand Your Bible.* Downers Grove, Ill.: InterVarsity Press, 1973.

Stott, John R. W. *Understanding the Bible.* Minneapolis: WorldWide Publications, 1972.

Tenney, Merrill C. *New Testament Survey, Revised.* Grand Rapids: Wm. B. Eerdmans Publishing Co., 1985.

Who Are We?

Discipleship Publications International (DPI) began publishing in 1993. We are a nonprofit Christian publisher affiliated with the International Churches of Christ, committed to publishing and distributing materials that honor God, lift up Jesus Christ and show how his message practically applies to all areas of life. We have a deep conviction that no one changes life like Jesus and that the implementation of his teaching will revolutionize any life, any marriage, any family and any singles household.

Since our beginning we have published nearly 100 titles; plus we have produced a number of important, spiritual audio products. More than one million volumes have been printed, and our works have been translated into more than a dozen languages—international is not just a part of our name! Our books are shipped regularly to every inhabited continent.

To see a more detailed description of our works, find us on the World Wide Web at www.dpibooks.org. You can order books by calling 1-888-DPI-BOOK twenty-four hours a day. From outside the US, call 781-937-3883, ext. 231 during Boston-area business hours.

We appreciate the hundreds of comments we have received from readers. We would love to hear from you. Here are other ways to get in touch:

Mail: DPI, One Merrill St., Woburn, MA 01801
E-mail: dpibooks@icoc.org

Find Us on the
World Wide Web

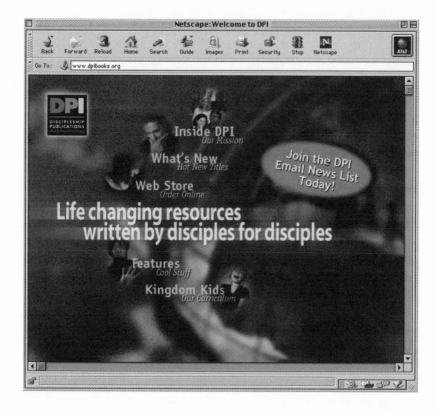

www.dpibooks.org
1-888-DPI-BOOK
outside US: 781-937-3883 x231